Winning The Game: Getting Started With Conversion Rate Optimization

Copyright © 2021 by Alexander Rådahl, RÅDAHL

ISBN 978-82-93915-00-3

Dedication

This book is dedicated to the love of my life, Edward. He has been by my side for the whole process of writing this book, and I'm so grateful for him. He's always there to support me when I need it, no matter what crazy idea I have next. Whenever I need help with something, he is there, willing and ready to do whatever I need! You are indeed a fantastic person that deserves all the best in life.

When I first started writing this book, he was so supportive and encouraging. He always pushed me to do better, even when it felt like nothing would ever come out of the work that I had put in. When things got rough for me or discouraged with my progress on the book, Edward never stopped believing in me! You are indeed a fantastic person and friend. Thank you for always being by my side!

When I got the idea of this book, I had barely started writing my articles, and suddenly I wanted to write a book. Maybe a little cocky attitude, and now that it's over, I realize that there's a lot that's going on in writing a book. I think you were very aware of the amount of work I had ahead of me, but you never discouraged me from doing what I wanted. Yes, you keep me accountable for what I have committed to and always tell me to finish what I've started, but you never tell me it's not a good idea. You let me be me, and by having you in my life, I have already won the game.

Thank you for being with me through everything and helping me along the way.

Table of Contents

Preface

In the many years I've worked as a UX designer, I've learned several key lessons to help put your website conversion optimization CRO) on the path to success. But I've also struggled to gather a bigger picture of how CRO plays when a team works together. Is the UX designer's responsibility? The marketer? And I've found it vague. In my world, it should be a joint responsibility. Hence writing this book.

After a lot of trial and error, I've concluded the winning formula for my clients and me. This is a formula I'm going to share with you in this book.

In the first part of my book, Winning The Game With UX Design & CRO, I will explain how CRO can be used as an effective tool for increased sales and profit. In the second part, we will examine conversion rates from both a financial and a user's perspective.

In the last part, I will show you how to put together a winning strategy on your website. It will be more theory-based than the first two parts of the book, mainly because there are many theories and competing views - but all with some truth (not too small). So instead of attempting to say which one is right, I will show you how to create a winning strategy for your website.

In this book, we will only look at the essential elements of CRO and UX design - many books go into detail on these topics separately.

I would also like to mention a companion book I've created based on Winning The Game. I have created a workbook where you can practice using these methods and better understand how to use them in real life. You can get a free copy on my website, radahl.no, or order a physical copy here.

Alexander Rådahl

Alexander Rådahl
Oslo, Norway.
20th of October 2021.

The Winner Effect: How Success Changes Our Brains

The Winner Effect is a powerful phenomenon that can be defined as "the tendency to become more successful in the future, simply by having won something in the past."

Winning a competition is like winning the lottery. When an animal wins, whether a fish or a human, there's a spike in testosterone and dopamine that changes its brain structure over time, making it more intelligent and more confident than before! Cognitive Neuroscientist Ian Robertson says

"success and failure shape us more powerfully than genetics and drugs." [1]

When you're winning in chess, sports, and business, your brain chemistry changes in drastic ways, this change in chemistry is called the winner effect. John Coates's book The Hour Between Dog and Wolf examines how Wall Street traders who win more often than they lose experience substantial hormonal changes, which make them more likely to succeed in the future. Ian H. Robertson also writes about how winning can be better adapted for educational purposes and serves enterprises. Both agree that success changes our brains.

With this theory in mind, I wanted to write a book that would set the reader up for success. Winning The Game with

UX Design and CRO is built upon 10+ years of experience and feedback on what literature is missing in the market. There are not many books on this subject, and most are created to promote a company or lack insight into how UX design and CRO play an equally important role in increasing conversions.

With this book, I will help you create a plan. A success plan. A plan to win. A plan to grow your business and increase conversions.

Introduction

You know that feeling when you're trying to think of a creative idea for your website but don't seem to get inspiration? You spend hours on Pinterest or scrolling through Instagram, and nothing speaks to you. I've been there too! It's frustrating because it seems that everyone else is successfully getting their designs into the world, while all you end up with is a bunch of sketches pinned on the board that you'll never use.

I was at my wit's end when one day I stumbled across an article about conversion rates and realized I was approaching things from the wrong perspective. All these articles telling me not to do didn't help me grow my business - it was difficult to collect an adequate stream of what I should do.

In this book, I will share a guide to UX design and CRO. UX is about improving the user experience for your website visitors by optimizing your website's conversion rate. CRO is about increasing conversions by testing different elements on your site to find what works best. In this book, we will discuss how to start as a UX designer or develop into a senior UX designer while also looking at the business side of things like CRO to be successful regardless of the industry you are in!

Even if you have just started as a UX designer or are currently working as one, CRO can help strengthen your skills and increase the size of your business.

1.

WHAT IS CONVERSION RATE OPTIMIZATION, AND WHY DOES IT MATTER?

Conversion rate optimization (CRO) is the process of identifying what makes a visitor buy and then applying those principles to other visitors. [2] CRO does not only improve your conversion rates, but it also reduces your bounce rates and helps make your site easier to navigate through, so it's easier for visitors to find what they're looking for.

Data provides insight into how changes on the website affect the conversion rate. However, there are many additional factors, including UX or UI design, that could impact conversion rates. Understanding these variables can give you an idea of which departments need attention.

The question in the minds of most marketers when they think about CRO is, "How do I make people buy?" The answer is not so simple. Conversion rates vary depending on the type of product and industry you are in. Nevertheless, five main principles will make every website better convert: clarity, simplicity, credibility, urgency, and social proof.[3] With the right combination of tools and techniques, you can efficiently pump up the conversion rate for your business for the customer you work with. The key is to create a complete picture of your customers, their patterns, and the user experience.

Some benefits of focusing on increasing CRO can be: [4]
- Increase revenue and customer acquisition
- Get your visitors to buy without little to any effort

- Dramatically increase engagement rates
- Know which aspects of your site work best with visitors, and optimize for even better results

It's easy to make your website more conversion-friendly. Following this guide for improving CRO should leave you with a streamlined, well-designed site that will convert visitors into customers at an increased rate.

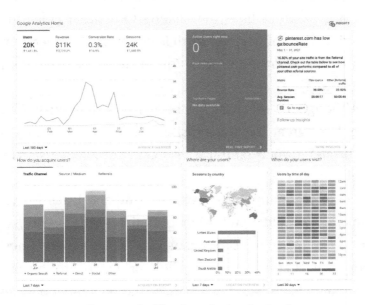

Data can come from tools like Google Analytics.[5]

Why do you need to optimize your website for conversions?

The design industry has changed drastically in the last decade and shows no signs of slowing down. In the past, designers focused primarily on everything visual: designing logos, creating brochures for customers, and advertising in magazines. Today's designers are expected to master more than one set of skills - from coding to content creation to analytics. The unfortunate truth is not every designer knows how to do everything well (or at least as well as its competitors).

Although in the past we have focused exclusively on designing a great-looking website or logo, today's design can be considered successful if it also generates conversions for your business.

There are many ways to gain traffic and leads for your business. Without conversion optimization, however, you lose a lot of potential business. UX designers should familiarize themselves with CRO principles to create a better and clearer user experience that generates business. Good UX designers can combine their aesthetic talents to create a beautiful and user-friendly interface that works well for the company.

For one customer, I increased their conversion rates by 15% with some simple measures. The company makes $150 million per year. This is an increase in revenue by $22.5

million. That does not even include the fact that they save much time on content production and friction in their purchasing process, saving both the marketing and customer service team considerable time and money. [6]

Google Analytics and other eCommerce business analytics platforms have shown the right optimization strategy for customer experience can be a make-or-break factor for any online store. Implementing responsive design, A/B testing of page layouts, creating engaging content assets to attract conversions, and optimizing checkout pages with payment methods will increase conversion rates by 300%. [7]

Examples of companies that have increased their conversion rates through CRO

Many of the best examples of conversion rate optimization (CRO) come from companies that may not be immediately associated with CRO or even a great UX design. These include brands like Airbnb, Shopify, and Amazon. It's no wonder these brands know their target market so well they can focus on specific aspects of the customer journey to improve conversions and revenue.

Later in the book, we will go through a few case studies on how different companies have improved their CRO and UX. These are not just old companies, but these modern heroes have used top-notch techniques to show you that they know what's up!

In the meantime, here are some remarkable examples of how familiar companies have achieved better conversion rates:

- **The Sims 3/EA Games** - Improved Value Proposition causes 128% more visitors to register for games. [8]
- **Intuit** - Increase conversion rates by 211% through the introduction of a proactive chat function. [9]
- **Crazy Egg** - Raised the conversion rates of their website by 64% with video. [10]
- **AMD** - Boosted the rate of people sharing their content on social media by 3600%. [11]

Why are businesses investing in CRO?

Have you ever visited a website and found yourself lost on the homepage because there were too many different options? You're not alone. It is easy for companies to be carried away with their creativity, but in most cases, this is not what people want when they come to your site.

The design industry is changing, and customer experience optimization has become a critical factor in success. With CRO, companies can better understand their customers to offer them the best possible experience.

Some reasons businesses invest in CRO:

- Improve the user experience.
- Reduce bounce rates.
- Increase in conversion rates.
- Be a more successful company.
- Identifying customer needs.
- Make the journey of your site visitors easier.

What is a Good Conversion Rate?

Conversion rates are such a crucial metric in e-commerce that you can make or break your business. When it comes to conversion rates, what is the best?

The average conversion rate for e-commerce stores in the US is 2.06% as of Q3 2020.[12] If you use all the strategies from this book, your conversion rate could rise from 3% to 4% or even higher. A 2% + should be the base goal for any online store. Once you have done everything effectively with these methods, it is time to move to more advanced tactics!

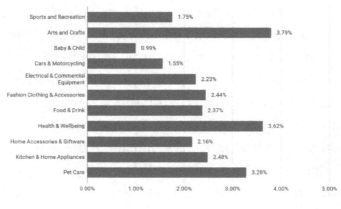

Average conversion by industry: Sports and Recreation: 1.75%; Arts and Crafts: 3.79%; Baby & Child: 0.99%; Cars & Motorcycling: 1.55%; Electrical & Commercial Equipment: 2.23%; Fashion Clothing & Accessories: 2.44%; Food & Drink: 2.37%; Health & Wellbeing: 3.62%; Home Accessories & Giftware: 2.16%; Kitchen & Home Appliances: 2.48%; Pet Care: 3.28%; [13] *Image from growcode* [14]

Conversion rates can vary depending on the industry, location, and other factors. Statista found that mobile conversion rates for Android and iOS hovered at around 1.94% in April 2021. [15] Such a low conversion rate could be that typing on smaller screens is more challenging, or that payment details and shipping addresses are harder to fill in.

However, regardless of why there is a lower conversion rate for those using mobile phones, marketers should know which devices could best complement their customer acquisition efforts.

Desktop users have a 1% higher chance of conversion. According to Statista, the average conversion rate between Windows, MacOS and ChromeOS is 2,97% from April 2021. [16]

2.

HOW TO GET STARTED WITH CRO

There are many ways to start with CRO as a designer or even a business owner. You can take courses on the subject, start reading books (like you do now!) or even talk to a CRO specialist.

I also recommend you have your website reviewed by an expert in CRO so that they can give you recommendations and tips for improvement.

If this book interests you, be sure to register for my e-mail list! I will keep updating it as new posts come out and any news/information to share.

How to get started with CRO - The basics

It's never been easier to get started with CRO! There are so many tools and resources, and it can be challenging to know where to start. In this chapter, we give you a breakdown of the basics: How do I conduct A/B tests, how do I measure my conversion rates, what tools are available to me, etc.

Some of the tools we would recommend:

Google Analytics

Many designers now use Google Analytics to help them understand their customer journey. Although it is crucial to understand the basics - what page people land on, how they navigate through your website - you can better understand conversion rates by looking at some more specific data points within Google Analytics. The tool is installed on some 29 million websites.[17]

See what's in it
for you.

Build a complete picture.
Understand your site and app users to better evaluate the performance of
your marketing, content, products, and more.

Google Analytics is a free web analytics tool that can track traffic patterns, traffic sources, and goal conversion rates in real-time. You can also track standard metrics, including sessions and sessions, and identify where visitors leave or which web pages have high bounce rates.

A tool is an indispensable tool for any business owner who wants to understand how their website is performing. Google Analytics helps you better understand your customers by providing insights into the demographics of those visiting your site, as well as what they are doing there. It's easy to set up too! You need to create a Google account and then add the tracking code to your website.

If you want to take control of your data, Google Analytics might be the place for you! While other tools offer similar features (many at a much higher price), Google has some excellent opportunities like segmentation, advanced e-commerce tracking, media insights, and more.

Google Search Console

We are all familiar with the Google search engine; what you might not know is it also has a tool for website publishers called the Google Search Console! [18] It's an SEO (Search Engine Optimization) service that helps site owners understand how their site appears to crawlers or bots on significant search engines like Google, Yahoo!, Bing, AOL, etc. This information will help you identify any crawling errors so that they can be fixed immediately.

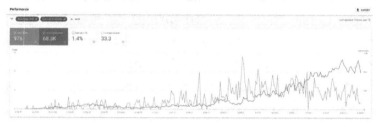

With Google Search Console, you're able to grasp more detailed stats on how users find your website and navigate your content based on their search term.

It goes without saying - I would recommend using Google Search Console daily when looking at your traffic source stats in Google Analytics. With this powerful little data point as one of your top metrics within Analytics, you'll have much better visibility into which keywords are driving people to your site, what pages they land on first, how much time they're spending looking around, and more. And because Google Search Console reports are so clean and easy to read, you can make informed decisions about which web content works the best for you!

Heap Analytics

Heap Analytics is a powerful tool that helps you understand your customers and what they do on your site. It helps you quickly identify problems and measure performance to make data-driven decisions about UX design in real-time. [19]

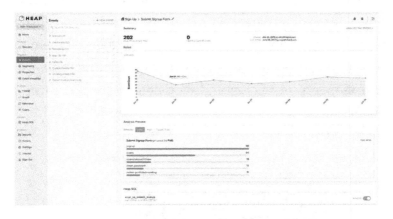

Heap can look a lot like Google Analytics, but it provides more advance insight.

With Heap Analytics, you can better understand what your users are doing on your site by tracking their activity and engagement in real-time through heat maps, scroll maps, click maps, and form analyses. You could use this information to quickly identify problems on your site, including broken links or unclear CTAs (calls-to-action).

Heap also offers A / B testing functionality, where you can test two versions of content to determine which version works better for conversions without manually implementing the changes.

Hotjar

Hotjar is a UX and CRO tool that helps you understand how your users interact with your website. You can visualize what they are doing on the site, watch videos of them using it, ask questions about their experiences, and get into the real stoppers to understand why people are not turning to buyers. [20]

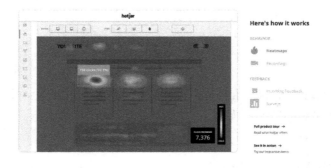

Hotjar offers a multitude of tools that you can use to understand the users.

Hotjar also offers A/B testing functions, where you can test two versions of content against each other to see which one works better for conversions without manually implementing the changes. There is also the functionality to view recorded sessions of users directly. [21]

Hotjar's UX and CRO features are beneficial for businesses to understand how users experience their site. With Hotjar, you can make UX improvements on your website without waiting for the next design project or hiring a UX agency. I always use this tool when I start a project to understand the everyday user experience fully.

GTMetrix

GTMetrix is a free web-based tool to measure how fast your site loads. The GTMetrix team has developed a proprietary algorithm that measures the load time of every single request on your website and provides you with a complete page speed rating, information about individual recommendations, and suggestions for improvements. [22]

GTMetrix gives you an excellent insight into the speed and loading problems of your website.

Speed is one key factor in UX: it affects conversion rates by up to 11%.[23] You also have no control over third-party providers like social media widgets or ads if they use their high-capacity servers rather than yours. A/B testing can help determine which provider works better, so there's less guesswork involved when making these decisions! GTmetric helps identify what may be slowing down different parts of your websites - including images, scripts, and hostnames. GTMetrix is a free UX tool that can help you measure how fast your site loads and where to start with optimizations for CRO!

GTMetrix is a UX tool that can help you measure how quickly your site loads and where to start with optimizations for CRO!

Google Optimize

Google Optimize is a free, powerful web analytics tool that can be used to optimize your conversion rates on both mobile and desktop devices.

Google Optimize compliments all the other tools Google offers for insight into your users.

It provides insights into what people are doing on your site and what steps they take to convert. It also allows UX professionals like us to test different pages for an increased chance of converting visitors into customers or leads - Google Optimize lets you change content without making code changes! [24]

The information we collect from this software will help companies make data-driven decisions and thus achieve their goals faster than ever!

Optimizely

Optimizely is a design optimization platform that allows designers to create and test variations in their digital designs. It provides both qualitative data from user surveys and quantitative data, such as conversion rates. Some big names have used the tool, including eBay, Dolby, and Pizza Hut. [25]

Optimizely offers in-depth data about your users.

The benefits of using Optimizely are:

- Designers can get feedback on their creations before they launch them in the real world
- It saves time because you don't have to wait for responses from users
- You can ask questions about your product or service without having to use any other tools

Optimizing your website is not a one size fits all task. What works for one company may not work for another. Still, luckily there are many great tools out there to help you make the best decision about which optimization strategy will get you the most results in your particular industry. Check out this list of CRO tools and see what might be right for you!

Key takeaways

UX and CRO are important for companies of all sizes, but the UX professionals at GTMetrics are here to help you make decisions with more confidence. If you're looking to increase conversions without making code changes, Google Optimize is an excellent option. Using any of these tools will ensure you have a head start in the game and can close more sales.

Winning The Game

The three types of CRO strategies

Does your design process lead you in the right direction? How can I know whether or not my design is successful?

With CRO and UX design, there are endless possibilities. Just like any new field in its infancy phase, there is still so much to explore and research to discover. For a young industry space with unlimited innovation potential, I encourage you all on your journey as boundary pushers who lead this pioneering profession of our time!

In my CRO strategies, there are three types:
- UX optimization
- A/B testing
- Funnel analysis

Each has its advantages and disadvantages, so it is crucial to choose the best suits you and your business needs. Let's look at it more closely!

UX optimization

The term UX optimization is a bit of an oxymoron, so we have to break it down. The two words combined can be understood as "the process of making something more user-friendly or efficient," which is somewhat true, but the word has no official definition, so we should look a little more into it. [26]

When it comes to making something more user-friendly, there are many ways to do this. You could make the layout less cluttered or colorful, so people know where they are going and what they need from the website. If someone is looking for information on how many calories are required per day, a critical button should be placed above the fold[27], rather than way down a page with tons of other buttons - which will help them get their answer faster. The point is when we think about UX optimization, we must consider not only "user experience" but also the impact that our decisions might have on "efficiency."

You also need to remember it is not just about improving the user experience but also understanding how people will use your product. It is important to remember that UX optimization is not a one-off thing. You have to analyze and change your design to keep it relevant constantly.

Funnel analysis: Why it is essential to measure success

Success is the best way to measure what you do right. If you do not measure success, how do you know if your efforts are worth it? The tricky part is to figure out which metrics are most important for your business.[28] Here are some questions to ask yourself when deciding what matters:

1. What does my audience care about?
2. How do I want them to feel?
3. What do they need?
4. How do I want them to behave?
5. What am I trying to achieve with my UX design or CRO efforts?

The goal of a UX designer is not only to solve the problem but also to create something people like. It is crucial for you as a UX designer to know what your users care about and how they will feel when they interact with them. Once you understand this, you can start designing to achieve those goals. Your focus should be on finding out who your target audience is and figuring out which metrics are most valuable for measuring success - regardless of conversion rates or engagement levels.

This often begins with the funnel analysis, and what is a funnel, you might ask? A funnel is a process in which a person takes one action and then moves on to the next. This could be the flow of a user from landing on the page until they buy a product or registers for a service.[29] The UX designer's goal with this type of analysis is to determine where users drop off at specific points in the process.

The conversion rate (or CRO) can also be considered a way for UX designers to measure the funnel's success. How to measure the success of the efforts in UX and CRO depends heavily on the type of business you run or work for.

More often than not, specific tools are used to make this type of analysis. I mentioned some of them earlier in the book, and I will touch upon them later.

The conversion rate is essential for UX designers to assess the success of their efforts. The goal of the UX designer is not only to solve a problem but also to create something that people like, which starts with understanding what users care about or how they will feel when they interact with it.

A/B testing

In its simplest form, A/B testing compares two versions of a webpage or application to determine which version works better. [30]

In UX, A/B tests are often used to determine which design variation of a website works better. Common goals in UX are to maximize conversion rates and minimize the time spent on individual tasks, such as browsing through products or navigating categories.

A/B tests can be used at various stages and help a UX designer determine which direction. UX designers can use A/B tests to assess which UX design patterns are more popular and implemented more often.

If we look at CRO and A/B tests, it is the perfect tool to determine the most optimized design and funnel flow for a higher conversion rate. [31]

What are the first steps in a successful CRO campaign?

CRO campaigns are about one thing: conversion. If your goal is to increase conversions, you must take a step-by-step approach that will lead you down the path to CRO success.

Often it starts with looking at the data you have already collected through various tools and insights within your team or organization. This could be Google Analytics, talking to the sales or marketing department, or directly with previous buyers.

It is essential to do research and better understand your customers before you start trying CRO strategies. What are their needs, what do they do now? How do we make them happier with our products or services?

Find out why they don't convert by asking:
- Where is the bottleneck?
- What are the UX issues?
- Do they know about all of our features and benefits?
- Are we targeting the right people with ads or offers that do not appeal to them?

Once you have discovered these findings, it will be easier to create CRO campaigns that meet your specific needs.

One example I discovered when I asked myself, our users, and the team these questions were that many people believed the checkout process was too complicated. It would be better if they could speak directly to a sales representative who could help them. The data we collect allows us to know more about what happens in your product. It is worthwhile to take some time to do this basic research before you start!

After researching what customers need, we should start thinking about solutions to the problems. Often it can help create different personas or user stories for the issues you have discovered. This will give you a better understanding of the customer and give us other solutions.

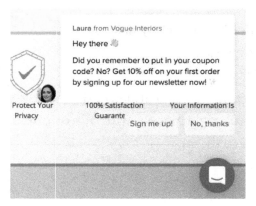

By setting up a chatbot at the right time for one e-commerce client, I increased their conversion rates by 5%.

Start brainstorming about how to solve these problems:

- What UX elements could we use to make sure people know they're on the right product page?
- How can we simplify the checkout process for customers who don't want to contact sales?

These are just two examples of questions you and your team should ask yourself to tackle the problem areas. In our case, we added this chatbot, which was timed right based on the data collected by customers via tools like Hotjar.

The UX design process is often divided into steps (as I will show later in the book). First, you have to put together the right team and do some user research. From there, your next step could be to develop different ideas for solving the problem you discover in the research phase, also known as ideating or brainstorming! Once you have some good ideas, it is time to prototype these designs so that users can test them. After trying it with customers, you want more feedback from other people in your team before deciding which one will become the final design.

The importance of A/B testing

Do you ever feel your work is not good enough? Are you questioning how well people will react to it in the market and wondering if all this time and effort is simply a waste, or worse, a complete failure? Well, there's a way to find out, and this tool is A/B testing! We have already touched a little bit on A/B testing, but I wanted to detail how it can be used in a successful CRO campaign.

Just a refresher on what A/B testing looks like:

A/B testing is a process that involves randomly showing 2 (or more) different designs to your audience and seeing which one performs better. This can be done on landing pages, social media posts, or any other type of marketing material.[32]

In an A/B test, when the user lands on a page or clicks through to it from social media, you randomize which design is shown. Once they've seen both methods and completed some action (ex: clicked "buy"), we randomly assign them again. This continues until enough people have viewed each variation of the experiment to see what performs better with our audience - this might be whichever version gets more purchases or any converting factor that is important for your business. The process can be repeated repeatedly for different versions of your website or marketing material so that you know what will work best with your customers.

I often see that working with A/B testing can significantly increase the conversion rate as you use real-life proof of what is shown to the user, not just a subjective meaning.

This is a different example of one customer I worked with on a home decor website, where we ran the same experiment and had great results!

I worked with a home decor e-commerce customer who wanted to know which pop-up for their newsletter would increase their conversion rate. They had some thoughts on design and incentive. One was a small gift with the first order, the second was a 10% discount, and the third was a combination of the two. I then decided to create an A/B test with their email marketing software to compare it, and we could observe a clear trend:

- **Gift only**: Converted 2% of the time
- **Discount only**: 0.62% conversion rate
- **Combination**: 8% conversion rate

We thought it would convert better with the gift and discount, but we were also afraid that might be too much information to give at once. We had no idea how dramatically different our conversion rate could have been.

Common mistakes that can be avoided by using the right CRO strategy

With the rise of digital marketing, it has become easier for companies to compete and hear their voices. Not all companies, however, take advantage of this opportunity. Some companies still make mistakes that can easily be avoided with a bit of planning.

Save time and money on the CRO's efforts by avoiding these mistakes:

1. Not understanding what your goals are for your campaigns.
2. Thinking of CRO as a solo project, not part of a larger plan.

3. Not testing different types of messages in other channels.

The rise in digital marketing has allowed all businesses to compete. However, not every company takes advantage of this opportunity and still makes mistakes easily avoided with a bit of planning. Digital marketers have recognized how important CRO is for their success and recognize it as an integral part of every campaign, not just another project on the list.

Key takeaways

The first step in CRO is the identification of the desired conversion rate. What are you trying to convert? It could be a purchase, an e-mail registration, or any other type of action that benefits the business objectives of the company. Once this is determined, you would have to think about what steps could help achieve them, and how these changes can affect customer behavior during their visit to the site. They can also retain visitors who have not yet made up their minds, while driving others to those crucial final touches, like adding items to shopping carts or, if appropriate, completing the checkout process. This requires a mindset of CRO thinking in planning and designing the service, and we have touched on some of them in this chapter. Moving forward, we will examine how we can use these tools while designing the user experience.

3.

HOW TO DESIGN FOR CONVERSION RATES

Designing for conversion rates can be a challenging task. It is essential to understand your audience and what they need from you because it will affect how we develop their experiences. In the last chapter, we explored various methods and tools to start with CRO. In this chapter, I will spend more time applying these methods to real-life and show you how I, as a UX designer, use this in my daily working life and help customers win.

In this chapter, you will learn:

- How to understand the user psychology of conversions
- Use of design to increase conversion rates.
- How copy plays a significant role in design and conversion rates.
- Tack-ticks that you can quickly implement and get immediate results from.

Understand the psychology of conversion

In the design and marketing world, conversion is a big deal. We spend time and money creating content that encourages people to subscribe to our newsletter or purchase our product. But how often do we take the time to understand what makes people want to convert?

- How often do you think about the needs of your audience before creating a campaign?
- What type of information do they want when they visit your site?
- Do you know what their questions are before they are asked?
- Most importantly, do you know how these factors influence conversions on your website?

If not, it might be worth creating content and advertising to understand better what motivates someone and the psychology behind it, to make sure you give them exactly what they want and need.

Take the time to understand your customers' needs, so you can create content that convinces them to engage with your brand!

The world of UX design is a proper art form. Designers must understand the needs and desires of their audience and simultaneously create an aesthetically pleasing layout that increases usability. Essentially, two individual goals are in mind: to make people's lives easier by presenting them with something they can use intuitively, without having to think too hard about, and to increase business through conversions. But don't forget that you want your work to create a fascinating experience. So when someone visits one page after the other, they are thrilled because everything looks cohesive rather than randomly thrown together.

With CRO, it starts by analyzing data from live site traffic using Google Analytics or any other similar analytics tool. You then use best practices in behavioral psychology, including split tests of various headlines, images, call-to-action, etc., which we will get into later in this book to create the most optimal user experience that meets your business goals. CRO is much like UX design, but it focuses more on the data and uses it to optimize your site for conversions.

Methods to understand user psychology

How do you know what your users think? Well, design psychology can help. I will detail the principles that guide my daily work and show how they apply to realistic scenarios. As a UX designer, I am often expected to read people's minds (not literally), understand precisely what our customers want and need, and then design a product that meets those needs - this can often seem an impossible task. Still, luckily, with these principles, it will be much easier!

Principle of Least Effort: Make your users think less

The Principle of Least Effort states that people will take the path or make an action requiring the least mental and physical energy.[33] In other words, the less you ask your users to think about what they are doing to use your application, the better! This is an excellent principle for UX designers because it can help them understand why some design decisions have been made; if there was no consideration given for this principle, more work might need to be done.

The design process is an iterative one, meaning you will make changes and grow over time. This may not be an issue if your app was only meant to last for a short while, but in many cases, that's not the case. When considering updates or redesigns, it's essential to keep this principle in mind because users are likely to get annoyed with having too many changes made without their knowledge; after all, they interact with the interface on just about every platform, so UX consistency is critical! [34]

Designing an app can seem like something you'll never finish - even when everything looks perfect, there might still be some tiny detail left undone, which could cause problems down the line. With constant client feedback and multiple testing sessions, these problems can easily be avoided by following a few easy steps for clarity and design continuity.

It's no surprise that people are always seeking fast and easy solutions with digital content. This principle is the guiding force behind UX design, which is why society now

Zalando.com uses this concept of broken down checkout very well!

demands flawless user experience on both desktop and mobile devices more than ever before, as this accounts for a substantial share of consumption of content.

Cognitive principles are the natural way that humans interact with digital devices.[35] To explore this connection, psychologist and cognitive scientist Susan Weinschenk has studied how psychology can be applied to UX design to work best for a human's brain. [36]

How to use it in everyday social psychology

Designing websites and apps is, in a sense, an ingenious form of communication. Understanding how we think on all fronts and perceive patterns as they unfold is essential to this generation's UX designers.

Here Grammarly uses a demo document to help you get started.

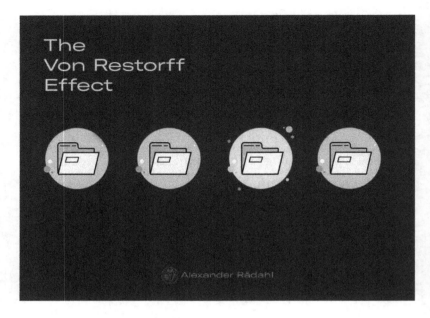

The Von Restorff effect visualized

Understanding how humans perceive and react to design is crucial for any sound designer. When developing a site or app, qualitative analytics are vital in giving you insights into what users do when interacting with your product. By integrating these findings into how we create our designs, designers can build something that truly resonates with people's needs.

Von Restorff Effect: The heart of UX Psychology

The principle was named after the German psychologist and philosopher Hedwig von Restorff.[37] Von Restorff's Principle[38], also known as The Isolation Effect, Predicts that the different ones will be more memorable when there are many similar objects because they stand out from all other identical things. Designers often use this to improve usability for their interface by giving users a prominent call-to-action to take action with. It's also used to study memory processes by manipulating the degree of similarity between two objects and observers' performance for discriminating them. The principle is so prevalent in design it has been made into its wordmark called the "Von Restorff effect."

Designing interfaces according to this theory can make interfaces easier for people who have difficulty distinguishing objects. [39] For example, a user with dyslexia might find it difficult to differentiate between the text for "submit" and "cancel." Designing these two buttons with some visual differences will make interfaces easier for users who need more time-consuming information processing.

Designing interfaces is a delicate balance of getting inside your users' heads and making their experience as positive as possible. Sometimes this means being creative with fonts, colors, or shapes to complete specific actions. If you're giving them a long-form but it's too difficult for them to see the current step they should be on, provide bullets

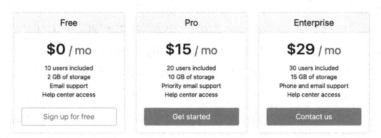

Here is an example from the framework Bootstrap where they used the color of the CTA to guide you towards the plans that will earn money, compared to the free plan.

that show progress so they know how much further there is left before completion!

We can't just design an interface without considering what our users will think about it-- after all, we are designing something right in front of their eyes every day when we use technology at work and home.

The better our input tone reflects these nuances, the more we'll improve overall usability by emphasizing specific information or highlighting critical steps.

Differentiating your plans by making them different shapes, sizes and colors will catch a user's attention. [40] If you want to show all of the offered projects unbiasedly, make sure they're similar in size/shape/color so that no plan is more favored than others.

We have to consider how our brains work to design an interface that will be useful and effective.[41] This is called cognitive psychology, which studies the human mind and brain functions to make better interfaces for humans.[42] The Von Restorff effect is one of those concepts from cognitive psychology that can help us create a more usable UX by using visual cues or highlighting important information on the screen.

However, the Von Restorff effect can work against you if something goes wrong. Apple Music wasn't great when it first came out[43]. People across the internet attacked it for being messy, hard to use, and bad at its job - which is not surprising in light of how well designed every other product has been from this company up until now! While some people report that it's gotten better over time since launch with many new features added each year, including Beats 1 radio stations as well as an all-new design makeover on iOS devices, Apple music will always have a poor reputation burned into them because they didn't get off to such a good start due entirely to their incompetence.

How to use it in everyday design psychology

Von Restorff's effect can be used in various ways to make our lives easier; check out these four!

1. Using **bold** and *italics* to highlight key text or points we want people to know more about makes it easier for the user to scan what you want them to see. [44]

2. **Enriching images with subtle details not found in the image itself** - leveraging our attention towards the parts of your design that hold more meaning will help users understand and appreciate your product's features much quicker.

3. **Playing on nostalgia by creating reminders of a positive event from the past** - usually done using color cues, illustration style, typography, etc., that matches up with something related to their history. [45]

4. **Including something unexpected in your design (a twist)** - will increase engagement with that specific part of the design because it creates curiosity within users which then makes them want to understand why they see this new item/ detail etc. [46]

These Von Restorff effect techniques are just some ways designers use psychology in UX Design.

Hick's Law: An essential law for every UX designer

Hick's Law[47] clarifies that how long a person takes to make decisions depends on the number of choices they are offered. The more options you present, the longer someone will decide because their cognitive load has increased significantly. Providing too many options at once can stifle

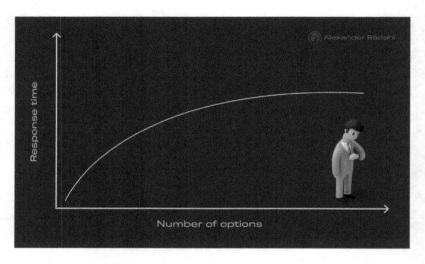

The more options the user has, the more time it takes to make a decision.

user experience as there becomes an unnecessary level of complexity in your product.[48]

One way UX designers have found for new users not to be overwhelmed with all those different functions available when using apps is through onboarding programs: these short tutorials teach them what buttons do what so that they don't needlessly click around or search aimlessly throughout your app looking for something specific; rather than having a feeling like "I should know where I want to go" but then not knowing where to go. [49]

When to use the law: Change blindness

The design of an app should be tailored for the needs of its users, something every UX designer knows, and what one user might find intuitive could overwhelm another with too many options at once or make them feel like it's not worth their time to explore because they're lost in all those choices. [50] To overcome this challenge as UX designers, you need to figure out which features your audience will use most often and provide easy shortcuts for everyone else. There shouldn't be any cognitive overload when trying to navigate through the app interface. That way, someone can have a more pleasant experience using your product without feeling frustrated.

The more complicated your decisions, the easier it is for your brain to get overwhelmed.

When you're under pressure and things go wrong, all of those quick-decision making skills are gone in an instant because stress has taken over. [51] It takes time - sometimes a lot of extra time - to recover from that after something stressful occurs. That's why when response times are critical, Hick's Law should always be used: keep the choices limited, so there isn't too much input coming at once which will make decision-making quicker without having tunnel vision or getting overloaded with sensory information. [52]

How to use it in everyday design patterns

Hick's law is perfect for simplifying significant, complex processes. With this rule in mind, as a UX designer, you can break down the cycle into smaller steps to keep from overwhelming your user with too much information at once. For example, suppose you're designing a payment system that has three screens. In that case, one showing cart details and another introducing delivery options before asking about account creation-you'll be able to give users all of the necessary info without making them feel like they have too many choices at once or needlessly scrolling back through pages on their screen.

The simple rule states that the more options you offer to a person in a system, the longer it takes them to make decisions. This generally occurs because people are unable to process more than one thing at once. In other words, we tend not to think about two things simultaneously and take in information from both of these sources.

Instead of adding any unnecessary steps or screens into your user experience design - which would only slow down decision-making even further by introducing new choices

Winning The Game

for users to sift through - try breaking up tasks with ease, so there is less input required on their part, from deciding between sizes and colors (say for shoes) where each size has its screen giving all relevant info without having to scroll back to the top of the page.

Serial position effect: One of the core design principles

The serial position effect[53] is a cognitive bias that dictates our ability to recall, recognize and organize data in a list. When participants in experiments are asked to identify or acknowledge items from a list, they do so better when presented at the beginning than at the end. For example, you might be more likely to remember the first item on your grocery list than one towards the end of your shopping trip. [54]

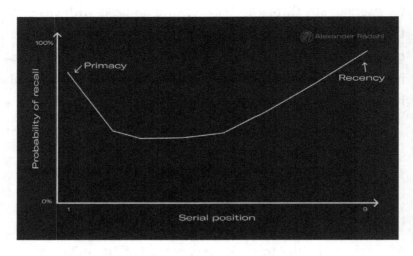

Visualization on the Serial Position Effect made by me.

Hermann Ebbinghaus, a German psychologist from the late 19th century, coined this phrase based on profound short-term and long-term memory studies.[55] These in-depth studies were further developed [56] by psychologists B. Murdock (1962) and Glanzer & Cunitz (1966). The experiments resulted in two vital concepts: primacy effect, which states that items studied first are more likely to be remembered than those learned later;[57] and recency effect, where information at or near the end of the learning list during an experiment has better recall when tested shortly after as opposed to memories not seen for weeks beforehand.[58]

Why is the serial position effect a thing?

The confusion may arise because participants have difficulty assigning an appropriate retrieval context (i.e., "line" vs. "list") for an item if it appears too far after one or more interfered items in memory. In other words, they may experience interference from those previous items when cued with later ones.

This effect may occur because people generally take more time to process information appearing at the beginning or end of a list since they expect it to be most meaningful. The brain shifts its focus when processing data, so anything processed first is considered salient and attention-grabbing--and will therefore resonate more powerfully with our overall memory for that event.

For example, one study found[59] that word order impairs sentence recall. When participants were asked about each sentence only once, instead of twice as usual (with an interval), they recalled fewer words toward their original positions but more within later places in sentences.

With 50% of the sentence remaining, the recall was facilitated by last words but inhibited by earlier comments.

The findings suggest that word order affects how we encode and retrieve items in memory--because people remember more information when they're cued with later ones.

Primacy effect

The primacy effect is based on discovering that an individual will recall items, assets, or information from the start of a list.

For instance, research has shown that when people try to remember something from a long list of words, they are most likely to recollect those terms at the beginning instead of further down. [60]

Recency effect

The Recency Effect is a concept that contradicts the Primary effect. Instead of recalling information from earlier in one's experience, the recency effect theorizes that people remember what they see last with more clarity. This model relies on short-term memory and is prevalent within courtroom settings as well. Studies show jurors are far more likely to recall or agree with arguments put forth by attorneys if those statements occur at the end rather than the beginning of argumentative information (or even during it). [61]

How to use it in everyday user experience

The way an interface is designed can significantly impact the user's perception and recall, which needs to be carefully crafted. As we mentioned earlier, two phenomena should be focused on: primacy effect (the items at the beginning of a list) and recency effect (things at the end). By understanding how these effects work, you can create more decadent designs for your interfaces by focusing on either end of this spectrum - primacy or recency. [62]

Here are some quick tips:

- **Provide accessible and relevant information** - provide the relevant information when the user needs it, don't overcomplicate things.

- **Use easy-to-recognize cues** - With the addition of dynamic signals to your user interface design, you'll make it easy for users to remember information and minimize cognitive strain.

- **Don't make the user recall all the time** - It is believed that the human attention span can only retain five pieces of information at any one time.

- **Critical and essential information should be at the beginning and end** - The primacy and recency influence how we perceive information. It is necessary to highlight the most crucial information at the beginning or end of your interface.

Use persuasive design to increase conversions

If you want to increase conversions and grow your business, it is time to integrate persuasive design into your marketing. The truth is that conversion rates are about psychology, not technology. [63]

The power of persuasion in designing a website or app applies in the subtle tricks that can be used to influence users without even recognizing that they are persuaded. [64] We have already touched on some of these nuanced approaches in the book. Designers use these tactics every day, but if you want to maximize the effectiveness of your designs, it is essential to learn how!

To help you get started, I have prepared a list of the most effective persuasive design tactics that can be used to increase conversions to your website or app.

1. Use recognition over recall to create a more familiar and comfortable user experience. [65]
2. Users who spend significant time on your site are naturally motivated to take specific measures. Scarcity is a strong motivator in the conversion process to push them to take action. [66]
3. Build credibility by drawing on existing authority with testimonials or social proof from previous customers. [67]

Here is a great example from Amazon showing me what I recently viewed while browsing their website.

4. When designing interfaces, it is essential to consider the status quo of users and their state of mind. [68]

5. Provide appropriate but achievable challenges to make users feel they have done something that brings value while using your service.

6. When designing user interfaces, you want to give the user a clear path to your goal. One way is to close off detours by nudging the user on the "right" approach you have planned for them. [69]

Big companies are always looking for new ways to make you feel more at home. Therefore, Amazon and many other e-commerce websites use recognition all the time so that when you return, you can pick up where they left off - finish your order or give suggestions of things from previous visits that might interest you now. [70] Recognition is promoted because it comes with the ease of knowing that you don't have to remember any information about the products you've seen or where you've found them. Amazon takes care of it for you and therefore encourages you to pick up where you've left off or bought the items you've been browsing for a while.

Persuasive design is a crucial UX principle that can be used to increase conversions.[71] It's about understanding how your users think and then using subtle tweaks in UX design principles to influence their behavior on your website or app. Understanding the power of persuasion will help you create a more familiar, comfortable UX for your visitors, so they feel at ease when making decisions online.

What you need to know about copy, calls-to-action, layout, and more

We all know how important it is to have an attractive design in the design of a website, but what about content? Content can be as crucial as ensuring that people stay on your site long enough to click on these call-to-action buttons and make purchases. These trees, copies, calls to action, and layout is often thought of separately or even by different teams. [72] But we must understand the complex relationship between them; they play together like peanut butter & jelly!

All about the copy

Your website's copy is its most important feature. The copy allows you to convey your message more effectively, persuade prospects to act, and generate higher conversion rates. [73] Many companies seem to forget when redesigning their website that copy plays an essential role in how well your company ranks on Google search pages[74]. It also contributes to organic traffic and the length of time someone stays on a website before leaving or becoming a customer.

The copy on the website should be persuasive and convince visitors that the product or service offered is worth their time and money. If it is not convincing enough, traffic from search engines will decline due to less time spent on your website. Conversions will also fall, as users are not persuaded by what they see on the screen. Finally, but most importantly, the customer's lifetime value decreases, leading to lost revenue for your business! [75]

When writing the copy for your website, you can follow some known models like PAS [76] and AIDA [77] to convince users that these problems are significant enough to be addressed.

- **PAS (Problem, Agitate, Solution):** Start by identifying problems your product or service can solve for your customer. Then describe how these problems affect the life and business of the customer. The final step is to position yourself as a solution to your problem with statistics, testimonials from satisfied customers, case studies of success stories, and anything that gives your product or service an advantage over the competition. [78]

- **AIDA (Attention, Interest, Desire, and Action):** This model is about grabbing a user's attention by targeting their pain points. Then getting them interested in learning more about how to solve these problems, making them desire your products or services in such a way that they feel they will improve their lives, and finally encouraging them to take action by calling the toll-free number or adding items to a shopping cart. [79]

Lastly, don't forget about your call-to-action buttons!

The button: Call-to-action

Once you have explained the problem your product solves, make sure you include a CTA (call-to-action) that gives users an answer to what they should do next. [80] The most important part of this process is to ensure that people buy into your solution and get it as quickly as possible!

The CTA should be prominently displayed on the website, and users should know exactly what they should do. The text of your call-to-action buttons should clearly state you want them to act. It is not enough to simply write "click here" or something similar, making people assume there is nothing important behind this link.

The button should be placed above the fold, but under your text about the problem and solution, or in other words, at the top of your site, as visitors can see it first when they visit your website. [81]

You will also notice there are different types of buttons depending on whether you use text or graphics:

- **Text only** - clickable link with plain font; looks like "continue reading" without more details than necessary to persuade someone to act.
- **Graphics + text** - the fastest option, as visitors don't have to read too much to understand what the button does. The icon or graphics also guide the users to the button.

It is essential to make the CTA button clear and easy for users to understand. The solution should be presented in a way that tells them what they need to do next, like buying a product or downloading a PDF to solve their problem.

How things look - The layout

What's the difference between a good design and a bad one? Is it just about aesthetics, or is there more to it? [82]

A good layout will present your content in an organized, visually pleasing way and ensure that every word on the page counts.

A good design is easy on the eyes while still being informative and precise. Bad designs distract from what you're trying to read by cramming too much information onto small spaces or using distracting images, colors, fonts, links, etc.

Looking at studies and data on how most users navigate a website or an app with their eyes, we can get a clear path to how we should go about designing the layout of the product.

There are two essential things we should keep an eye on when designing the layout:

- Eye-tracking studies. These studies track what people look at on a website and how they move their eyes along each page to glean insights into how users navigate content on a site, where they get stuck, or where they might hesitate before deciding whether to click through or not. [83] This is helpful for UX designers because it tells us which parts of pages need more attention in terms of design and placement within the context of the hierarchy (e.g., navigation vs. body copy). Eye movement can also tell if people scan your images or text-like headlines as soon as they see them, so understanding eye movements will help you decide if things like headings have the right color and size.

- We also want to make sure that the site is fully responsive, as many users are now using their mobile phones and tablets for browsing. It's not just about how your website looks on an iPad or Android device anymore. It's about optimizing it for all appliances, so you will still be able to engage a user who clicks through from a phone when they're at home in front of their computer. [84]

In the end, your design is only as good as the content you use to back it up. So if you're looking for a way to make sure that people stay on your site long enough to click those call-to-action buttons and take action in some form or another, start with an enticing idea about what they'll find when they get there. You can't just have attractive graphics without any substance behind them; after all, we live in a world where everyone has access to high-quality images at their fingertips, thanks to Google Images and other similar services. Content matters!

And while not every business owner will be able to invest time into writing blog posts or finding related articles that are worth sharing on social media sites like LinkedIn, Twitter, or Facebook, you need to be able to show your readers that you're keeping up with industry trends.

Design for mobile devices and tablets

Mobile devices and tablets have been around for some time now. The first iPhone was released in 2007 and the iPad in 2010. With these technologies, we can do everything from checking our emails to playing games on the go. Designers must create websites compatible with mobile devices so that people can enjoy their content, no matter where they are - or what device they use.

The importance of designing a website that is accessible and easy to use on any device cannot be underestimated! With 54% of all Internet traffic coming from mobile phones in the first quarter of 2021[85], there is no option not to design with mobile phones in mind. Smartphone users are more likely than desktop users to abandon websites that do not load quickly enough. [86] Therefore, responsive websites - those that automatically adjust their content according to the user's screen size - are crucial if you want visitors to be happy and engaged with what they find on your site.

Remember that not all devices are created equal, and you may need to create a different version of the website for people using mobile phones with small screens. You can do this by using responsive web design or creating two versions of the same page - one optimized for desktop users and another explicitly optimized for mobile phones.

Create a sense of urgency with scarcity tactics

There are many choices in today's world. But when it comes to making decisions, people are often influenced by fear of missing out on something extraordinary. This is called the "scarcity" mentality. [87]

The tactics of scarcity include:

- Limited time offers.
- Coupons tailored to the buyer, which expires.
- Scarcity messages such as "time are running out."

These tactics create urgency in our minds, encouraging us to act now rather than later and dramatically affect the conversion rate.

For example, if you shop at Nordstrom Rack and see a pair of shoes you love, but they don't have your size in stock - what do you do? You might buy them anyway, even if they're not your actual size because they will be gone tomorrow!

If a customer is insecure about the product or service, they will likely not buy the product or service you're selling. 94% of online customers do thorough research on prices and discounts before they believe and find cheaper alternatives, even if you have an incredible offer! [88] This means it is essential to limit the time of your deals to create urgency earlier - people love saving money, don't they?

The scarcity mindset is so powerful that it can be applied to any product or service. By adopting this tactic, consumers can perceive products with limited availability as higher quality and more valuable. Product placements on TV are an excellent example, as an actor looking for their favorite candy bar, as they talk about how excited they are to finish the next season of their show. From this point of view, we might think - "I have to get my hands on one!"

This tactic works because when people see something hard to find, they fear missing out if there is still too little time. It is human nature: our minds always want the best, and we are afraid that if we don't have it immediately, there might be no more.

In a world where there are so many options for everything - not just candy bars - this can take its toll on our mental health. It is only natural to feel like you missed something enjoyable if you could have had it but didn't. For this reason, scarcity tactics work: they remind us that time is limited (or running out) and encourage us to act now rather than later.

Offer free shipping on your site or in-store pickup

It is a common misconception that the offer of free shipping takes away your profits. In reality, it is the opposite. When you offer free shipping on your site or in-store pickup, customers are more likely to purchase because they are not worried about paying for their order and have nothing else stopping them from making the purchase. [89]

The psychology behind free shipping is that it makes customers feel they're getting a bargain. Increased happiness from this feeling can lead to higher customer satisfaction and word-of-mouth advertising, which will increase your bottom line in the long run. [90]

In addition to creating incentives for customers who were not sure of buying something upfront by reducing purchasing barriers (shipping costs) and increasing their likelihood of completing a transaction with you, it has also been shown that free shipping creates loyal shoppers. This means presenting them with a quick and painless checkout process, where they are not asked to enter their payment or delivery details several times.

Provide social proof by displaying reviews, testimonials, and ratings from customers

In e-commerce, there is a fine line between creating interest and scaring away customers. To optimize your e-commerce conversion rate, you need to find the optimal balance of social proof from existing customers that encourages customer conversions. [91] Social proof can come in many forms – reviews, testimonials, endorsements, ratings, and more. Online buyers are more comfortable purchasing from an e-commerce store when they realize that their friends and family have done so. Social proof is, therefore, an essential component of conversion optimization.

According to one study[92], 27% of customers use reviews and social proof to determine which company to support. By contrast, only 24% of consumers never consult a company's online evaluation before purchasing. Customers nowadays have many options, and reviews can be an essential tool to narrow them down and increase your store's conversion rate.

Social proof can be a powerful tool for businesses and consumers alike, but it is essential to remember two sides. If your Facebook feed or Twitter account has negative social media posts about your product or service, you may fall victim to this phenomenon – discourage potential customers from trying out the products or services you sell.

The problem worsens with online reviews published on social channels, where every person's voice is strengthened by contacting companies directly and publicly with their concerns. This means you have to respond quickly when dealing with complaints about goods. Otherwise, it may appear you are not taking complaints seriously.

Companies can use positive social proof to their advantage. If you receive an excellent review on TrustPilot or another site, consider putting it on your site – perhaps as part of a dedicated review page or the product page. You can also consider incorporating it into your social media strategy to show your customers and reputation.

Consider using pop-ups or other forms of intrusive marketing to capture leads

I know what you think - indeed, there are more ethical things to do than follow the tactics of those pesky pop-ups and other intrusive marketing campaigns. I'm with you on this, but hear me out.

Pop-ups and other forms of intrusive marketing are undoubtedly working. They grab your attention, interrupt you from what you do, and make it difficult to ignore them. But how can it be applied effectively? What are the best practices for using these tactics in a way that does not annoy your audience?

From a UX perspective, pop-ups are one of the many ways to interrupt your audience and attract their attention. An example is when you scroll through Facebook on your phone - there is nothing more frustrating than not to scroll down without having an ad appear above where you were trying to go.

For this reason, some brands have decided against using them because they do not want to annoy users with something that does not match their brand identity. These tactics can completely discourage customers from interacting with the site or app in the future because it feels like spamming people for no reason (which it is). But if used correctly, this type of advertising can be highly effective and lead to severe results.

Best practices for pop-ups:

- Test, test, test! Make sure you test your popups, the timing, the design, and the message. The best way to do this is by A/B testing (you can use a tool like Optimizely for your convenience).

- Instead of focusing on selling something, focus more on capturing leads and building relationships. This will create trust with consumers, which could lead them to buy from you later on. It takes time to build trust with consumers, so make sure always to publish high-quality content and interact on social media.

- Use images and visual elements to capture the attention of users. Don't let the pop-up be full of texts, as it could turn them off instead of attracting their attention. Remember, you're trying to grab their attention quickly, so they don't scroll right by!

- Remember that UX is about solving problems or achieving a goal for your audience, so be creative!

A/B test and stop wasting money

A/B testing of a landing page is a beautiful way to understand which landing page experience will be most effective for your website. With A/B testing, you can quickly find the adjustments necessary to increase the conversions of your landing page and capture leads, get more customers and create a better user experience.

A/B tests can help convert more site visitors into buyers but also improve the values of your products or services. Once you have discovered a landing page form or design that works well, don't leave it as it is forever. After identifying a method that works for cheaper goods and services, A/B test it. You may discover customers are willing to pay a premium for more expensive options that appear to offer more perceived value with merely a few tweaks and continuous A/B comparison tests on your landing page.

Many people believe A/B tests are only for forms, photos, and simple text when it comes to your site. Nevertheless, you can test any messaging or campaign to get the correct type of visitor by changing their landing page! The slightest change could make a massive difference in determining which combination attracts more leads and turns them into visitors who decide what they want at all costs. Don't hesitate; it's better to act now and start testing than wait until your competitor grabs the spotlight from you with their landing page!

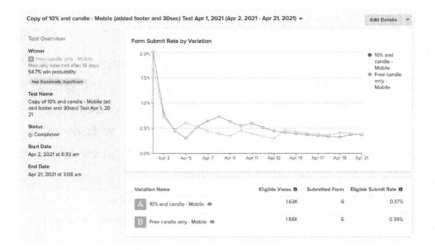

A/B testing can be a valuable tool when you want to test different forms or messaging on your landing page or website.

While more data is typically preferable in testing, this is not always the case with A/B tests. Although early findings should be taken with a grain of salt, you do not need millions of page views to find out which versions offer more significant results for a landing page that generates few conversions daily – you can still rely on patterns in the data you have and start the landing page optimization immediately! Even if you're creating or generating only one or two sales per week, find out what conversion brings most customers so far without spending too much time waiting for a lot of visitors.

We touched more upon this technique earlier in the book!

Tips for designing a good landing page

Designing a conversion landing page is no easy task, but with these tips, you can create a compelling landing page for your business:

- Create tailored pages based on the personas of your potential clients and buyers.
- Create an emotionally compelling and persuasive headline. Your headline should immediately attract the attention of your potential customers without being too wordy or over-the-top!
- Develop clear and concise value proposals with bullet points.
- Use testimonials and reviews to create social proof.
- Include a clear CTA (call-to-action).
- Create a compelling offer that encourages your customers to buy. Your marketing should be so irresistible that they don't want to say no!

If you follow these tips to design a landing page, the person who sees it (or has positive results) becomes the winner!

Winning The Game

4.

COMMON MISTAKES DESIGNERS MAKE WHEN THEY STAY WITH CRO AND HOW TO AVOID THEM

Winning The Game

We are all looking for quick fixes and shortcuts. If you are a designer who is just getting into conversion rate optimization, I will give you some secrets that will help you avoid common mistakes.

We are often testing without a clear conversion optimization strategy.

Testing is a crucial part of their design process for many. But when it comes to conversion optimization, we often do not have a clear strategy that guides our decisions and actions.

One way to make the most of your tests is to use an experimentation framework, such as A/B Testing for Websites or Lean Startup's Build-Measure-Learn loop. These frameworks will guide your decision-making and help you optimize your success before taking action on any new tests. In "Getting started with CRO: The Workbook," I have compiled several methods that you can use to set your goals. You can get a free digital copy at radahl.no, or a physical copy can be obtained there!

Lack of structured test processes

"I need a tester to test my design. I don't know what they're supposed to do, but let's just do it anyway."

This is an all too common sentiment in our industry, and it's hurting us. For designers, getting feedback is crucial for the iteration and improvement of their work. But without a structured testing process throughout the design life cycle, we often find ourselves without any idea how to get that feedback from testers or where to go next. It is time to take control of this problem by establishing standard practices and testing processes and understanding how our role fits into the enormous scope of product development.

I've always been a fan of testing. I have seen that it gives me immediate feedback on my work, improves the quality and consistency of my design process, and even makes me a better designer.

Not knowing how to track and evaluate your conversion rates

... is one of the most common mistakes designers make when they start with CRO.

What can you do to prevent this mistake? Here are three tips:

- Track your conversion rates by using a third-party tool such as Google Analytics or Visual Website Optimizer (which is free!)
- Find and track metrics that matter to your business, not just those that seem important from an individual UX perspective; these may include revenues, enrollments, or completed trials
- Keep it simple! Test only one variable before moving on to another to eliminate variables and identify what causes results changes.

These guidelines give you the best chance of getting feedback without making any other costly errors along the way.

Testing small sample sizes leads to inaccurate conclusions

Most people do not realize that trying small sample sizes leads to incorrect decisions about your design. [93]

The reason this happens is statistical significance: if you test something on small sample sizes, there is no way to tell whether the result was due to chance or not.

So if I were designing a button that said "submit" and tested it on ten people, I wouldn't conclude what color wrote better without doing tests on other colors.

The takeaway is that you have to test your design on a large enough sample size to conclude.

For this reason, if I wanted to find out which link color works better for my blog, I would have to compare it to every other possible variation of the same link color.

There are ways to solve this problem, such as A/B tests and multivariate tests, as I mentioned earlier in this book.

Designing without knowing your customer

Designing without knowing your customers can be a complicated business. Every designer needs to know their client to create an engaging design tailored to the user group. The hardest part of the process is to figure out who you are designing for; it is not as simple as deciding on an age group or target group.

Understanding your customer's business and target audience is a critical component of the user experience design. Are you designing an e-commerce site? Or are you working on an app that is used by thousands of people every day? If you can't answer those questions, who knows what to expect from the final product!

Knowledge of the customer allows the designer to create experiences that make them feel they are getting exactly what they need from your product or service. This creates satisfaction in both users and customers.

Here are a few ways to learn who you are designing for:

- Ask users or buyers of your service or product.
- Talk to competitors' customers and get to know who they are and what they miss out on in the competition.
- Create personas - Check the chapter on UX research to find out how to create valuable personas.
- Survey your users - Join this effort by directly interviewing some of your users to create a quantitative and qualitative overview of your users.
- Research competitors and current trends in the industry - Conduct your market research!
- Watch user testing sessions or check analytics data for usage patterns.

5.

THE IMPORTANCE OF UX RESEARCH IN THE DESIGN PROCESS

UX research is a critical component of the design process and should not be overlooked. It is essential to understand your user before you start a project, to ensure that you design with them and their needs in mind.

The most common misconception about UX research is simply another form of market research or focus group. This couldn't be further from the truth! Market research can give us insights into what people like and do not like about specific products but does little to explain why they feel that way and how their preferences compare with other potential users.

UX researchers spend time observing real users in their daily lives - whether at work or on a competitor's website - to understand better who our user base is and what they want out of a product or service.

In this chapter, we will discuss the importance of UX research and how it should be integrated into your design process.

The most important thing to remember about UX research is that this type of experience will vary from person to person depending, for example, on age or gender. Therefore, you want to strive for a universally balanced understanding of what people are looking for when navigating your building product.

In this chapter, we will deepen how to conduct proper user experience research and how it can help you improve your conversion rates. I would also recommend keeping your

"How to Get started with CRO: The Workbook" close, as I will discuss many methods outlined in this chapter as exercises in the Workbook!

You can get a free digital copy at radahl.no, or a physical copy can be obtained there!

What is UX research, and why do we need it in the design process?

In my opinion, most designers have a strong sense of how they want their product to function and what features they want. But designing without research is like building a house without an architect's blueprints! The UX designer examines the behavior and needs of users to create a coherent design that encompasses all sides of the process. So there is no getting away from talking to, researching, and looking into who your users are and what their needs are.

In recent years, the process of doing proper UX research has been put on the agenda for companies that want to create a product that resonates with their customers and users. Through this research, UX designers should create a design that reflects how people want to use the product, not only what they think is the best way to use it.

This chapter examines some examples of why UX research is so essential for developing successful products and provides you with some general guidelines on how to carry out appropriate UX research. Much has been written about user experience research. However, many companies still do not know precisely what this means or why we need it to make our designs more effective and increase customer satisfaction rates.

The importance of user testing

Designers and marketers are constantly looking for ways to improve their work. It is often difficult to identify the flaws in your design, and it can be hard to know where you could have improved things. The best way to find out is to test your plans and ideas with real people, so user tests should be an essential part of any designer's process. [94]

Before you spend hours on a new project, you have someone test different parts of it as you develop it.

Some of the things to test:

- Navigating through the site.
- Sign up for an account and log in.
- Testing of various features of the site/app.

Some of the best ways to perform user tests are:

- Invite people to test your website or app in exchange for feedback.
- Create relevant surveys for what you are testing, and try relevant users, preferably based on a person.
- Perform A/B tests of the features you want to test. [95]

- Friends, family members, colleagues, or others who could be potential users of the site/app can try to navigate through it while watching their experiences.

User tests can help designers solve problems with UX design by improving customer satisfaction rates and finding ways to increase conversion rates. It helps them make informed decisions about how they want to enhance techniques before they spend hours working on something that might not work as well as they expected. When done correctly, user tests give valuable insights into what customers are looking for, so the designer can quickly iterate and get traction. [96]

The different types of UX research

The importance of thorough user research before designing a product or service is widely recognized, but it is essential to know which types of study will be most helpful for your project. Below I will discuss some top UX research methods and their respective advantages and disadvantages so that you can make the best decisions for your project!

So let's get right to it. Here are some methods that I like to apply during UX research and the benefits of using them in your processes.

Market insight

Market insights are the most common type of user research because it is necessary to know what your competitors are doing to stay ahead. This is also crucial for learning about new trends that may not have been popularized yet, so you can start incorporating them into your design before everyone else! [97]

Websites like Google Trends can give you a starting point to explore trends in the field you are currently working on.

Businesses can use various analysis methods, including competitive intelligence and market analysis, to get a head start on their quantitative research. [98] The former is performed by reviewing the analytics of competitors' websites, such as page views or conversion rates. At the same time, the latter can be done on social media platforms where customers post their latest purchases with hashtags such as #OOTD (Outfit Of The Day), giving an idea of what type of customer they are targeting and how well it works for them!

Advantages of market insight: [99]

- Provides valuable information about competitive intelligence.
- Explore new trends before the competition.
- It helps stay ahead of competitors and keep pace with design changes.
- It is easy to do for people without experience in UX research.

Market insight is crucial to UX research, as it provides valuable information on competitive intelligence, examines new trends before the competition, and helps stay ahead of competitors.

Personas

Personas are another type of UX research used when working on a new product or improving on a new one. They can be fictional or real, usually determined by the designer based on their own experiences and knowledge.

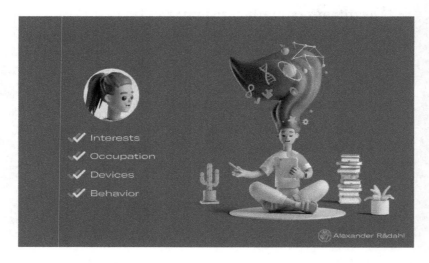

Personas can help you create an overview of who you are designing for!

These help better understand your user because they typically consist of information collected through interviews, surveys, focus groups, observations, and contextual inquiries. It is important to note that you should never rely on only one or two persons because they may not represent the entire group.

109

Advantages of personas:

- Improvement of the user experience.
- Help you better understand your audience with personas.
- Give you a better idea of who to create a product for and how to use it.
- Investigate changes to improve the quality of the product.
- Enhance empathy with your product.

Personas are an excellent method of user research because they allow users to be understood and the product to be made with empathy, which leads to a better user experience. I always use this as a critical component of my design methodology.

As an add-on to this book, I have also created a free-to-download workbook containing several tools you can use on your CRO journey. It also includes several templates for personas. You can go to radahl.no to get your free copy or buy a physical copy.

Usability testing

The best way to find flaws in your product is through usability tests. This type of UX research allows you to determine whether people can easily use it, what steps they take when using the app or the site if there is confusion about crucial features such as contrast and readability. Testing for weaknesses before launch will help ensure a solid customer experience on your website/mobile application! [100]

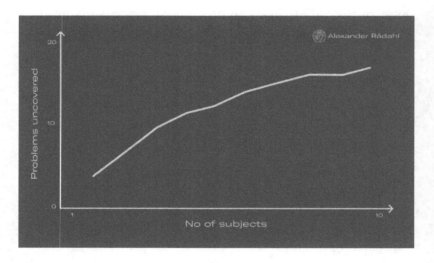

This curve shows a flattening of problems reported around 10 test subjects.

Usability tests are an essential tool for any UX professional. Jakob Nielsen developed the technique of 5-person usability tests. He argued that once one or two people are completely confused by the prototype design, little can be achieved by testing more subjects who struggle with an imperfect method.

"Elaborate usability tests are a waste of resources. The best results come from testing no more than five users and running as many small tests as you can afford," says Jakob Nielsen. [101]

Nielsen's point is that testing with five users, solving the problems they discover, and then testing them in a different group of five is better than performing a usability test on 10. In practice, these tests are carried out once or twice a week during development, when three to five people are tested in each round, and the results are delivered within 24 hours so that you can identify any problems before you implement them. He also notes that the number of users tested within a project can range from 40 to over 100. Research shows that user tests carried out by organizations typically involve recruiting 5 to 10 participants. [102]

Benefits of usability tests:
- Gain insight into how your website or app is used.
- Find and fix problems before they become problematic.

- Get more information about what users want from your product.
- Understand whether something needs to be rethought from the ground up.
- The results are highly accurate, as you get unbiased feedback from real live users.

We rely on usability tests to find errors in our product before it is launched. This will help to ensure a solid customer experience in the development you undertake.

Creating prototypes for user feedback and more

A UX prototype is a model that illustrates how the software will function and the experience it creates. A UX prototype can be made with wireframes, mockups, or other visual elements. The goal of UX prototyping is to avoid costly design and development mistakes by experimenting early and often. [103]

Prototypes allow users to grasp an idea in its most basic form before investing resources in building something that might be too complicated or not what they wanted.

You can easily create a prototype with paper, pen, and other tools for early testing. This is one of the best UX research methods because it is quick and easy to make prototypes! [104]

Benefits of prototyping:

- Fast, easy, and cheap.
- Simple for every level of skill.
- Allows customers to help shape your product without spending much money or time upfront.
- Creates better products with less risk.
- Improvement of the efficiency of early product design.
- Increases ROI because you don't waste resources on complicated products.[105]

Prototyping is one of the best UX research methods because it is quick, painless, and inexpensive. This allows your customers to help shape your product without spending much money or time upfront. Ideal for pre-launch tests so that you can optimize the success of your product at launch! Later in the book, I will go more in-depth about how you can conduct prototyping and the benefits of the different methods, so stay tuned!

User testing

This type of UX research tests whether your product meets users' needs, which is crucial in designing a digital product and belongs to feedback methods in the design process. [106]

User tests can show you whether any features need to be added and more by letting people use products with varying levels of expertise, so you know who your target audience should be. This method differs from usability testing because user testing focuses more on the features and how they work.

Benefits of user testing:

- It helps ensure your product meets the needs of users.
- It shows you how consumers use the product.
- Design support so that it can be both simple and intuitive

User tests help ensure your product meets the needs of users. This allows you to design a simple but intuitive product that consumers can easily use!

User interviews

User interviews are among the most trusted research methods in UX and one of the most commonly used observation techniques (at least in my arsenal of research tools).

These sessions with actual customers help designers and developers understand what users want and complement your qualitative research. Therefore, it is essential to connect with a diverse group if you wish to feedback on your product or service. [107]

Advantages of user interviews:

- Get an authentic understanding of what your users want.
- Find insight into pain points and desires that you may not have been aware of if you did not do this research yourself.
- Learn how to build better products and services by watching people use them.
- Improve your UX design skills.

User interviews are an excellent way to understand what your users want and need. They are a fantastic, affordable way to get feedback on your product or service.

Surveys

A survey can be used for many purposes, but one of the most popular is collecting data. There are two types: closed-ended and closed-ended surveys. [108]

Closed questions generate data for quantitative research that will help support your idea or decision. In contrast, an open question generates data for qualitative research that provides more details without being biased by answers given when you ask a direct question about a topic.

A standard tool in UX research is to examine people's thoughts on functionality, usability, etc., using qualitative and quantitative methods, depending on what information needs to be collected from participants. I would also say that surveys also belong to the category of feedback methods in the design process.

Benefits of surveys:

- Helpful in getting feedback on an idea or decision.
- Gain access to impartial data.
- A simple way to get feedback.
- Access to qualitative and quantitative findings.

User surveys are one of the best ways to get feedback on your product or service quickly and cost-effectively.

Focus groups

Focus groups are an excellent opportunity to get feedback on your products. They are like surveys in that they allow you to ask specific questions and collect data, with the added advantage of meeting people's reactions to qualitative information. [109]

Benefits of focus groups:

- Convenient ways to get feedback from your target group.
- Highly customizable and adaptable to different research needs.
- A friendly, non-intimidating environment in which participants feel comfortable giving their honest opinions.
- Cost-effective research methods.

- Face-to-face interaction with the respondents.
- Online interviewing is an excellent option if your product is not available in that country or language. (or we are in the middle of a pandemic).

The focus group is an excellent way to get feedback on your products. It's like a survey, but with more qualitative information, allowing you to communicate directly with potential customers.

Contextual Inquiry

Many people use this research method, but it could be a game-changer. This involves talking to customers about their experiences with your product and how they use it in different contexts, giving you an idea of the challenges users face in using your product. [110]

Combining this with focus groups and user tests can give them excellent insights into what is most important!

The benefits of contextual inquiries:

- Give you an insider's perspective on the user experience.
- Learn more about where customers struggle with your product.
- Understand customer needs and expectations from different angles.
- Create various ideas to improve the user experience.

- Contextual inquiries are an excellent way to get an insider's perspective on the user experience.

How to conduct UX research

Does your design research require a fresh coat of paint? If you want to learn how to conduct UX research, the best place to start is WHY, WHAT, and WHO.

Why do you carry out this study? What do you or your team hope for from the end-user's perspective, and what will be their goal after doing all this? These answers give directions for everything that comes next in a compelling user experience analysis.

It is easy to get carried away when you are excited about a project. Many designers underestimate the importance of conducting research. They jump into designing wireframes and prototypes without talking to potential users or researching their target audience's wants and needs. The best way to make your product desired by people is to do some old-fashioned market research!

We have talked a lot about how to conduct UX research, but the key is to know what kind of action plan you need to do thorough user research to create both a beautiful design and a positive user experience. Why? We want a balance between qualitative and quantitative research: one that ensures that we have sufficient data for both strategy and execution while bridging gaps between our target users on all sides.

Some critical questions you can ask yourself or your team are:

- What are the objectives of this research?
- What are you going to research and why?
- Who is your target audience, what products or services do they use now, and their competitors?

This information should help determine how to conduct UX research.

WHY

WHAT

WHO

Some general steps for a successful UX study include:

- **Define objectives** — brainstorm solutions with stakeholders and use the questions mentioned above.
- **Conduct user interviews** — collect qualitative data from potential users about needs and wishes.
- **Monitor customer service calls/online chats** — understand the challenges people face in real-life situations where they might need support.
- **Survey size (e.g., 100)** — quantitative analysis of responses collected by surveys or surveys that measure opinions, attitudes, knowledge, etc.
- **Create personas** — a fictional representation of the use /stakeholder used to classify groups and create empathy for end-users.
- **Design wireframes or prototypes (depending on the goal)** — understanding how design decisions can affect UX research
- **Ask questions in person** — get a deeper insight into what would work best with our target audience.
- **Test designs against goals and objectives** — validate assumptions by testing various solutions before making a final decision. This process may take some time, but it will lead to better results because the designer will have considered more options in advance.

- **Document the results of the study** — what were the most important findings? Have valuable thoughts or ideas been lost in conversations? Use a standard documentation tool so that everyone can see what is happening.

Performing a successful UX study is more than simply asking customers what they want and then giving them. You have to know their needs, why they have those needs, how often these problems occur, and whether the problem has been solved before. Critical steps in conducting a successful UX study include defining goals with stakeholders so that you can brainstorm solutions together and understand customer service calls/online chats. Therefore, you are aware of real-life challenges people face when using your product or services. Survey sample size to measure opinions about your company's products or services and create personas, as well as other fictional representations that represent different types of users within your target group(s). [111]

In summary, it is essential to carry out user research and have a structured plan with an end goal in mind. Conducting this type of UX research can help you create a better product for your target audience by understanding their desires and needs before designing the final product or wasting time on something that could be avoided at the beginning of a project. The key to conducting UX is getting answers as quickly as possible, so you know who will use your prototype, what features the end-user wants, and where the design team should focus its efforts from day one! [112]

The process will manifest differently depending on the case, the team, and how you want to work. But with the above example and the tools in the last article, you have a head start on how to conduct UX research.

How to conduct a user interview

Interviewing with users can be a challenge. One of the most important aspects of interviewing is to get to know your subject, your needs, and what you want from your product. [113]

In this part of the chapter, you will find examples of how I conduct a user interview to get the information I need to design a successful product!

1. Make sure you have a list of questions to ask

Questions can be a powerful tool in the design process, but they are not always easy to develop. The best thing you can do is have a list of questions ready to conduct user interviews. [114]

What should I ask in the interview? You might wonder, here are some examples:

- "What are all the things you need to do to do [task]?"
- "Guide me through [task], how would you do it?"
- "What are your thoughts on [problem]?"
- "Why do you think that [problem] is happening?"
- "What are all the things you have to do to get something out of the product?"
- "What do you think about this problem?"
- "Why do you think this is happening?"

2. Be aware of your body language and the way you're sitting

I don't know about you, but I'm a sloucher. It's how I sit when I'm at my desk, and it's also how I sit when I'm chilling on the couch. But sitting in a bad posture is uncomfortable for me and makes the subject you interview with uncomfortable. [115]

The two things we want to avoid when it comes to our body language are slouching and crossing your arms over your chest (also known as "defensive position"). Slouching makes us tired, while crossed arms make us feel closed in. In addition, both positions can also be interpreted as less interested or interested in what we are doing. It seems to be such a simple fix, but many people don't know they are doing any of these things until they're pointed out! [116]

3. Start with open-ended questions, then move on to more specific ones

We often have prejudices about a product, so ask open-ended questions to start the interview. To help them explore and think about the questions at hand, start with open questions that require more than a yes or no answer. [117]

Start by asking them their opinions or impressions of your product. This will give you an insight into whether they are interested enough in your product to explore its features.

The following are some examples of open-ended UX interview questions to ask:

- What's your first impression of this product?
- How would you describe how it works?
- Where do you imagine this tool in your daily workflow?
- Do you feel something is missing from the design/features/function of (product)? What might that be?

4. Write down any observations or insights that come up during the interview

If you are looking for a way to improve your interview technique, one of the most critical aspects of an interview is to take notes. This gives you something to refer back to during the conversation and helps write your report. You can also use programs such as Notion to organize your notes and reports for later use. [118]

5. Ask for feedback at the end of the interview, and be prepared to take notes!

When you finish the interview, it can be a good idea to ask for their feedback on how you conducted the interview. This can also create a less formal atmosphere where participants could share valuable insights as their guard is down. It also allows you to improve your skills for the next time!

6. Follow up with a thank-you email after each user interview is complete

How often do you thank a user after they have discussed it with you? I hope that the answer is always!

I have become accustomed to sending follow-up thank-you emails after each user interview to show my appreciation and offer any help if needed.

This simple gesture helps keep pace with the design process and makes the subject feel good about what they have just spent with you.

It is important to remember that this is not an e-mail in which you ask for feedback but simply a way to be thoughtful and kind in your interactions with others around design research.

Tools to conduct a user interview

During an interview, it is essential to stay organized. As you talk about more subjects, you may get a lot of information and confuse yourself with organizing yourself. That is when it is essential to have the right tools!

Some tips from me:

- Use a notepad to jot down notes. This will help you keep up with the conversation and record all crucial details that might have been forgotten at the moment.
- Have pens or pencils nearby to take quick notes. Please don't use your phone because it's more likely to be distracted by notifications, emails, SMS, etc.
- Bring separate sheets of paper if you need them for information gathering or data gathering. It can also be helpful to bring an extra set to create copies as required if you get dirty by filling in messy handwriting!
- While it is not directly a tool, snacks and drinks are also a nice touch.

I also carry these tech devices during an interview:

- An iPad or any other tablet to draw, take notes, or even give them examples.
- Headphones if I want to play them something from my phone.
- Portable charger if I want to do a more extended interview or session.

Tips to make the most of your time during the sessions

When you are in the interview room for user tests, you can do several things to make the most of your time. Whether you have an hour-long session and want to make sure every minute counts or are looking for new ways to speed up the process, here are some tips that could help you on the path to success that I apply during my sessions.

- Make sure you have snacks and drinks at hand. This is not just a courtesy: many people feel more relaxed when well-fed, so it can also be a productive time!
- Carry a portable charger if you are in the session longer or want to make it interactive (this goes hand in hand).
- Make sure to plan some time between each interview if some of them run long.

- If you have a long session ahead of you, make sure you take breaks between interviews so that your brain can get some time for recovery.
- Remember to open windows during your sessions to bring in fresh air to keep alert.
- Make notes of which specific questions worked well with certain people during each session and which patterns or themes emerged throughout the day. Whether this means writing down critical insights from the participants, creating post-it notes with the following steps, categorizing other observations under different headings (example: CRO), or taking detailed screenshots of something remarkable, this will help tremendously in the later development of UX changes. It might even be worth exploring how these techniques work.
- Bring your post-it for a creative outburst.
- If possible, have a whiteboard in the room so that you or the topic can draw ideas and show them.

Tips for conducting interviews with children and adults

The key to getting the most out of an interview is preparation. If you interview children, it is best to have a list of questions appropriate to their age group. Interviews with adults should be more accessible, but don't forget your notepad and pen!

Children are a joy to be around, and they have a great perspective on the world. But before you can ask them about their thoughts or experiences, they will need your help to feel comfortable.

Here are some basic rules that I set myself every time I go into an interview, whether it's children (or adults): [119]

- Keep your tone of voice conversational, not formal or intimidating.
- Use appropriate eye contact with the person you are interviewing.
- Do not ask leading questions - let them answer in their own words without prompting from you.
- Be mindful of body language - do not cross your arms or look bored.
- Keep an eye on signs that they are uncomfortable, and change the topic if necessary.
- Don't forget to ask about their hobbies, interests, and favorite things!

- Allow pauses between questions, as it may be difficult for some children to respond quickly or at all.
- Make sure you ask about topics appropriate for their age group.

The next time you interview someone, try to keep your tone conversational and appropriate for the topic. Remember how much eye contact you give them - some people may feel uncomfortable with intense eye contact! Don't forget to ask about your hobbies, interests and favorite things too! If they ever appear awkward or want to stop answering questions, change the subject instead of insisting they continue to speak. A professional but witty tone will make it easier for everyone involved in the interview process!

Questions to avoid asking in an interview

Not all questions are created equal some can harm your research project before it even gets off the ground! [120]

What is worse than asking a question that does not contain valuable information? Asking one that ultimately leads you down an unproductive rabbit hole from which you never emerge. In my opinion, the following list of questions are a few fine examples of what you should not ask during a user test interview:

- Would you like to use the old version of this site or the newer version?
- Was this the easiest way to get to that point? (implying this was the easiest way)
- Is that the best design?
- Don't you think that's an inadequate solution?
- Is this not just an annoying way of doing X?

How to conduct prototyping

One of the main benefits of prototyping is to get feedback and reactions from people who will use the product early in the design process. Prototypes let you investigate different aspects of UX design before investing in it and committing to a final plan. Creating paper prototypes early in the design process can also help identify problems or shortcomings before they become too difficult to solve later when the visual design has already been established in high-fidelity prototypes or even developed by your team.

Let us look at an example of the importance of prototyping early on. Let's say we're working on an app called "Homes Home," an app that shows you an overview of your home with essential details such as bills, scheduled maintenance, etc. This app would appeal to many user groups, from young adults with their first house to retired couples. Working with such a wider group requires a lot of user data and user research. You might find that a layout or design does not work for all users, and the team decides the homepage needs to be tailored based on who the user identifies as.

Making this discovery early in the design process saves the design team a lot of time for making the final mockups and the development team time. Imagine if this had been discovered much later when some development had already

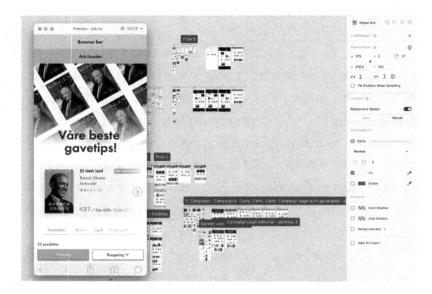

I love the prototyping tools that Adobe Xd offers, especially with its auto-animate feature!

begun, countless hours would have been lost, and design concepts would have to be discarded by the UX designers.

It is also worth noting that prototypes may not always be perfect and maybe miss some or all of the content that will eventually appear in a final product. Sometimes it's okay to have a prototype with no or limited functionality, but this should be decided case by case, depending on how much risk is involved and what can still reasonably be discovered from a preliminary design.

What are the best prototyping tools for UI/UX designers?

I'm asked this question all the time. The answer is not as clear-cut as you might hope because there are two basic approaches to prototyping, static versus interactive.

Static prototyping tools like Photoshop lend themselves well to the more traditional graphic design skills for creating layouts and logos. I have to note that these are not often used and, in my opinion, should not be used at all. Tools like Figma, Adobe Xd, are an excellent way to create a higher-fidelity prototype if you have the technical chops and want to bypass some limitations of a wireframing tool in your digital prototypes.

Interactive prototyping tools like Figma, Sketch, Principle, and more give you the whole package of the prototyping toolbox, from designing to animating elements in your high-fidelity prototype. These are the ideal tools for rapid prototyping that are interactive.

Static prototyping is often carried out in paper prototypes, which I will detail later in the article. This type of prototyping usually does not require prototyping software and will be in the low-fidelity league and cover only the essential elements of the interaction design. Paper prototypes are extremely useful when testing out new ideas, screen layouts, and product ideas.

How do I use prototyping software and tools in my design process?

Prototyping is a natural part of the design process when we're working with user experience design. It's a way to bring the best design ideas to life and also establish which concepts are feasible. The prototyping tools you use at each stage of the interaction design process will vary. We often refer to the design process in 5 steps, as defined by the Interaction Design Foundation: [121]

1. **Empathize** – Find out what your customers want. You should develop an empathetic understanding of the issue you're attempting to address, generally through user research.

2. **Define** – Identify the Needs and Issues of Your Users. It is time to collect all the information you have collected throughout the Empathization phase. You then combine your findings to identify the most critical problems you and your team have discovered.

3. **Ideate** – The goal of this stage is to challenge your assumptions and develop ideas. You are now ready to create concepts. As you have a solid foundation of knowledge from the earlier two phases, you can start thinking outside the box, looking for different ways to perceive the problem, and proposing creative solutions to the problem statement you made.

4. **Prototype** – Start developing solutions. This is a period of trial and error using prototyping tools, pen, and paper. The aim is to find the best solution for each problem that arises.

5. **Test** – Experts carefully evaluate prototypes. Although this is the final step in design thinking, it is an iterative process: teams often use the results to redefine one or more additional topics. As a result, you can return to previous stages to make further

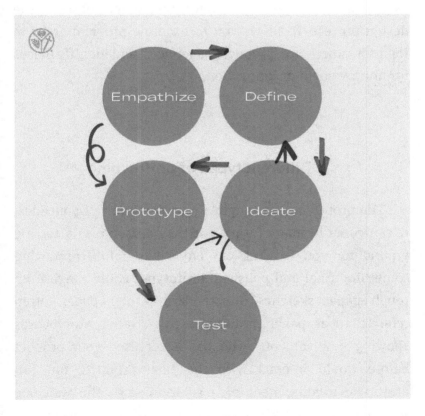

The design process as defined by Interaction Design Foundation.

138

iterations, changes, and refinements to discover or eliminate alternative answers.

These phases are mainly followed in the order described above, but we will always go back and forth between the steps as we discover new information that we must consider. You can find assumptions and biases you have toward your ideas, as well as insights about your users that you can use to improve your solutions or create new ones by prototyping and then testing those prototypes. Paper prototypes can be used as a form of research even before other phases in the design process. It allows you to examine problem areas in the user experience, products or services, and identify places for improvement or innovation.

Different types of prototyping

The prototype is a tangible representation of your idea. It can come in many forms, but they all serve as a testing ground for you to work out any kinks before producing something final and polished. Prototypes could range from rough paper sketches on standard printer paper, often referred to as paper prototypes, to narrative storyboards showing how someone who has never used your product before would interact with the final product. You can prototype a component of a solution (e.g., the welcome screen of your app) to assess this aspect of your concept.

UX prototyping can be performed in many ways, and it is essential to find the way that works best for you and your team to get to the final product.

Paper prototyping – The value of simple paper prototypes and low-fidelity

The most basic and low-fidelity prototyping process is paper prototyping. To do this, you first have to draw up a document that defines the user interface and then sketch out your functionality to mimic how it would work on a digital device. For paper prototyping, you can use any paper you want, as long as the layout and sketch reflect what you will eventually do on an app or digital interface. It is best to design these prototypes for design review with other people involved in the project, including stakeholders because they can point out things that may not make sense or contradict your original vision. The paper prototyping method can be invaluable early on, as you don't have to invest too much in creating it, and you can iterate quickly with your team.

Optionally create a wireframe

Wireframes are one of the most important elements of UX design. They are used to communicate how the final product will feel without color, graphics, or media and can be a key in early usability testing and to observing how the user flows through the product. Wireframes only use the layout and content for an idea and typically contain headers, logos, navigation menus, text input fields, and buttons. The wireframe is traditionally black and white, so it can be easily shared with developers who want to know where the text should go or what items they need to code. The purpose of a wireframe is to convey the hierarchy of the content of your website so that stakeholders or product designers can start making decisions about placement in the layout.

They can also be used as prototypes of higher fidelity than paper prototypes during user tests.

Storyboard prototyping

Storyboard prototyping is a type of UX prototyping that focuses on the user experience. It is used to construct a series of screens that show how a user's interaction with an app or website would unfold from start to finish. The prototype also includes functional transitions and exits, such as if you were on a roadmap and clicked on Ohio, the map changes to Ohio and starts in Cuyahoga County. This prototype is most commonly used in the early stages of design for creativity and brainstorming sessions but can also be used to test with users at any point in the design process.

HTML prototyping

An HTML prototype requires some more work but can lay the foundation for the further development of the product you are working on. With this type of prototyping, you can present a more natural-looking and feeling version of the final product. It also allows you to understand better how the product feels and get valuable feedback from users about it.

Wizard of Oz prototypes

A Wizard of Oz prototype is a type of prototyping that simulates the interactions with a system as if it were life. This type of UX prototyping carries the responsibility of a "wizard" who poses as the system and responds to requests from the user. The wizard can be remote or local and can take any form you want. The wizard interacts with a user by pretending to be a computer, a person, or an object responsible for creating the system. This type of UX prototyping is used for systems with many interactive parts, such as decision-making trees, slideshows, or maps.

User-Driven prototypes – The best way to prototype UX?

User-driven prototyping is different from other prototyping techniques in that you do not create a prototype to test people. Instead of creating a prototype to evaluate users, you ask the user to develop something that will help the team understand more about their customers. User-led prototypes are not intended to be used by users themselves. Instead, they are used to gain insight into the ideas of the user. What can I do to make airport parking more comfortable?

User-driven UX prototyping is an excellent method for creating unique ideas and concepts. The only thing you have to do before you start brainstorming in the design phase, or even in the early stages of product development, is talk to users about their challenges. Then it's time to put your thinking caps on. Outline the difficulties your users might have, and imagine the best possible solutions with your team.

Prototyping conclusion

UX Prototyping is a tool that can test UX concepts and get valuable feedback from users on what they like or don't like about your design. Consider using the various types of prototyping methods we discussed in this article, including Wizard of Oz prototypes, which help test more interactive systems with many parts, HTML prototypes, which allow you to present a much more natural-looking version of the final product, and User-Driven Prototype, where you ask an end-user their opinion rather than creating something for them. The best approach to verifying your ideas, learning about customers, and improving the user experience is to prototype quickly and often.

Common pitfalls that designers should avoid when conducting UX research

We've all heard the saying "measure twice, cut once," [122] and it's even more critical when designing a user experience. Research is a crucial step in the UX design process because it gives you an insight into how people currently interact with your product or service so that you can refine and improve what they are already doing. But there are some common pitfalls that designers should avoid in conducting UX research.

Listed below, you will find three points that I have discovered as the most significant pitfalls:

Lack of control groups

When conducting UX research, it is essential to have a control group to determine the validity of your results. We often design for two or three people and then try to extrapolate our findings outwards. This can be detrimental because we cannot accurately represent what the larger population would experience with our designs.

Not enough participants

The participants are the lifeblood of UX research. To understand their needs, you need a certain number of people who fit your target group to achieve statistically significant results. Too few participants, and you don't know what your users want from your product.

Too much time spent in one place

For a UX researcher, it is easy to get stuck in one area of research and not to explore the other avenues that could yield more fruitful results. For example, if you are interested in figuring out how people feel about your product on their phones, you could spend the whole day clicking on your app and completely forgetting to examine it on a tablet or computer. Or if you're trying to find out what motivates someone to buy a specific type of car over another, you might spend hours talking to them about why they want that particular car, rather than getting into details about what's going through their minds when they're looking at different vehicles online.

Conclusion

UX research is an essential component of the design process. It's not just about usability or what users anticipate, but also how they use it in different contexts, which gives you a better idea of the challenges users face when using your product. Contextual inquiries can monitor customers as they go through your UX and ask them questions to understand their needs and expectations from different angles. This type of research generates ideas for improving the user experience that you might otherwise have missed.

Your user is the most critical component of your design process. Understanding how they think and their goals will help you create a product that meets those needs. In this chapter, we have learned about UX research - from different types to why it is so essential in every project.

Now that you have several methods in your arsenal to conduct user research and plan a CRO campaign, it is time to look at some examples in real life.

Winning The Game

6.

CONVERSION RATE OPTIMIZATION CASE STUDIES

The goal of optimizing conversion rates is to increase the number of people who take the desired measures. It is not always easy to know where to start with CRO, but there are some CRO case studies that can help you get started.

In this chapter, we will examine four different case studies of CRO and discover what each company has done differently to improve its conversion rates by up to 200%.

Amazon: How they became the biggest e-commerce market in the world

Amazon is one of the largest retailers in the world, but they are not content with resting on their laurels. They know that to remain competitive and relevant, they must constantly experiment with new ideas and methods to increase conversion rates. To find out how Amazon has expanded its conversion rates, we will examine the improvements made in recent years.

Recommendation of the right product at the right time

Amazon has become a master of product recommendation. And it's no wonder it's increased sales over the years with the amount of data they have about their customers and products. They have found that combining a customer's past purchase history with their browsing habits maximizes the chances of making a sale.

In this way, Amazon not only recommends products based on what you are currently viewing but also suggests items that they think may be interesting or relevant to your shopping experience.

Marketing Sherpa analyzed e-mail conversion rates to determine what works best in the world of e-commerce. [123]

There were two types of campaigns: the general batch-and-blast approach and the Amazon-style targeted one, where offers are targeted and recommended to users based on factors such as interest. The latter was much better, resulting in a 208% increase in conversions.

Amazon's recommendation engine accounts for a whopping 35% of Amazon.com revenue[124], accounting for about 50% of the US online retail market.[125]

Amazon's "Your Recommendations" link takes you to a page with items recommended for you based on the data they have about you. This allows them to get their customers to explore new products and buy more. And yes, I'm into making my own wine outside of UX and CRO.

Amazon's UX and CRO strategy has been successful due to the amount of data about their customers. They use this information to recommend products based on previous purchases, browsing habits, and interests. Recommendations are also personalized using machine learning algorithms that learn from customer interactions with other people's purchase histories and Amazon's inventory.

Frequently bought together

Total price: $36.84

Add all three to Cart

ℹ️ Some of these items ship sooner than the others. Show details

☑ **This item:** Twin Bubble Airlock and Carboy Bung (Pack of 2) $6.75 ($3.38/Airlock)
☑ FastRack Auto-Siphon Mini with 6 Feet of Tubing and Clamp $13.10

"Frequently bought together" recommendations are designed to up-sell and cross-sell clients by suggesting goods based on the items in their carts or those they're currently looking at on a site. The idea is that if you've been shopping around, there's probably something else you want to buy too!

For this reason, it can be so difficult for competitors to compete against them because not all companies have access to the same level of user intelligence or aggregated data about what shoppers want or need at a given time. This allows them to keep up with consumer trends without having an endless budget for market research, as some of their competitors do - which ultimately makes their UX design and CRO strategies a success.

But if you look at Amazon and implement some of its methods on a smaller scale, you can also achieve admirable results in your conversion rates.

Building a personalized experience for your visitors continues in your inbox

Amazon has mastered the art of customer acquisition through e-mail marketing.

One way Amazon uses e-mails is to send discount codes or vouchers for future products in your cart. By incentivizing the purchase with a coupon, they create an emotional connection to their brand by making you feel you're getting something for free when you're paying less money than if you weren't on a promo code.

This tactic also helps them build loyal customers because it feels good to get a deal - especially after all the research and decision-making process into online shopping.

Make sure your checkout saves the customer e-mail as soon as they fill it in so that you can follow up with an abandoned e-mail and give them an incentive, such as a discount, to encourage them to pick up the items. If you personalize remarketing ads and campaigns with the proper segmentation and message, you can get up to 1,300% ROI![126]

Improving the checkout process will reduce the abandonment of the cart

According to Baymard Institute, the average industry standard for abandoned carts is a whopping 70%! [127] This is a lot of lost customers and revenue that you can quickly recoup with some simple optimizations. If we look at it in terms of pure dollars, it's $18 billion a year lost down the drain. [128]

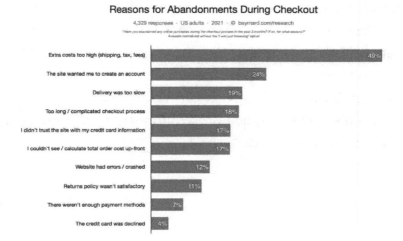

Reasons for abandonment during checkout from Paymard Institute.

44 Cart Abandonment Rate Statistics - Cart & Checkout - Baymard Institute. (2021). Retrieved 17 October 2021, from https://baymard.com/lists/cart-abandonment-rate

Another Optimizely study found that 68% of shoppers go to Amazon because they trust the site and what they will find there. [129]

Almost all major retailers are constantly working on making the checkout process as smooth as possible. Still, no other retailer has made it an integral part of converting new customers as Amazon - with "one-click" payments. With a click on a button next to your items in list view or search results, you can buy anything without entering payment information again.

Amazon has devised a clever way to help you check faster and more efficiently by using a multi-step checkout.

Various studies have shown that an excess of form fields can lead to a reduction in conversions. Indeed, a CRO company has been demonstrated that removing the phone number fields can increase its conversion rate by up to 48%. If possible, reduce any additional information and only keep the necessary contact details. [130]

First name

> John

Last name

> Doe

Street address

> House Number and Street Name

Town / City

> Albany

Don't bother with collecting customer details you don't need, adding more fields will increase the chance of the shopper leaving your checkout page.

You could use a multi-step sign-up process, like Amazon, to ensure conversions don't get negatively impacted. Marcus Taylor found that in some cases, the update of a company's checkout form to a form with several steps increased conversions by 743%. [131]

Later in the book, I will dive deeper into more general ways to optimize your checkout.

Do not make substantial design changes without doing your research

Amazon has been around for a while, and they know the value of taking their time to test and research what they should do to increase their conversion rates. They have not changed too much in the last ten years.

In 2011, this was a new design Amazon introduced. Not much has changed since that time when it comes to structure of the pages and user patterns.

If you are redesigning your website, don't make extensive design changes without doing any research first. It may be tempting to do something different and original with the new website's design, but this often leads to increased confusion for visitors who may not know how to find their way around the site or what they should do next. People are often reluctant to adopt changes in established experiences, and Snap Inc learned this the hard way when its recent redesign led to a drastic decline in revenue. [132]

Designing for familiarity is a way to keep users coming back for more - but how do companies know when to make changes? [133] It is important not to change your site too often so that it remains familiar. This is in line with Weber's Law of Just Noticeable Difference, in which the "difference threshold" or "just noticeable difference" is the slightest change in intensity that people can perceive. [134]

Set your focus on social proof

When you buy a product on Amazon, what do you typically do next after knowing the product specifications? If you are like the average e-commerce customer, you will immediately go to consumer reviews to find out what others have said about that particular product. A Baymard Institute study found that 95% of people rely on online opinions during their shopping process, which will help them make decisions about the products they are considering. [135]

Research shows consumers are more likely to trust a review if they see the number of ratings and reviews. [136] It has also been found that people usually pay attention to product titles, star ratings, customer photos or videos, and social media content about products when making online purchases. The Baymard Institute study showed that user-generated content in CRO is so important because it accounts for 95% of all consumer decision-making on e-commerce websites during their shopping process. [137]

Amazon does this well by building trust in its products,

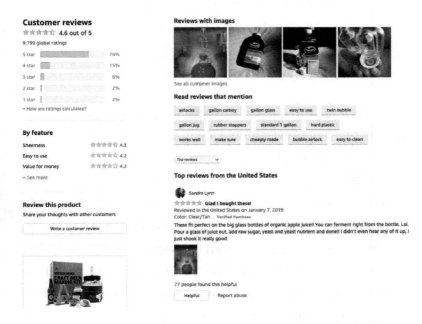

Browsing products on Amazon, I can get a good glimpse at genuine opinions of consumers of the product I'm considering buying. Users can upvote reviews and also share pictures and videos of the product.

and also in the context of reviews, and creating an incentive for users to leave reviews and become part of Amazon's review community.

Companies can use positive social proof to their advantage. If you receive an excellent review on TrustPilot or another site, consider putting it on your site – perhaps as part of a dedicated review page or the product page. You can also consider incorporating it into your social media strategy to show your customers and reputation.

Conclusion

We have much to learn from Amazon about CRO and UX. Amazon has been testing new ideas and methods to increase conversion rates for many years and will do so in the foreseeable future.

One of Amazon's main focus areas has been to create a personalized experience for its visitors. This is repeated in their inbox, with emails tailored to them based on what they have seen and have not seen yet, even though they might be interested in viewing it. This could improve checkout processes to reduce cart abandonment, which ultimately means fewer lost sales due to the inconvenience.

Airbnb: How do Airbnb's changes to website and platforms result in 150 million users?

Airbnb is one of the world's most well-known and recognizable companies. The company has grown significantly since its inception, with over 5,6 million listings in 100,000 cities worldwide and 800 million guests staying in an Airbnb property since last year. [138]

The design team at Airbnb continues to develop a fantastic product, and it is mainly due to its unwavering commitment to offering its booking platform a superior user experience compared to other services in the same space.

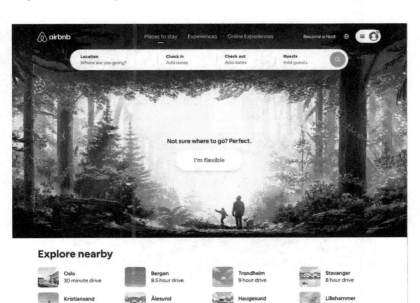

As an expert in CRO and UX design, I was always fascinated by the UX design process at Airbnb. What are some of the things that have contributed to their success? Here is my analysis of the critical factors in CRO and UX design, which has helped grow Airbnb over time.

But how have they been so successful?

The answer to this question may be Airbnb's changes to its website and platforms in the last ten years.

To understand what we are talking about here, it is essential to look back on its history and determine its change.

The front-page of Airbnb in 2012. Picture from UX Timeline.

In 2008, Airbnb launched its website with a static homepage that offered visitors to register for the service or post an apartment listing online. [139] This design was updated in 2012 but still looked comparable to every other typical site from that time, which is why it didn't take off as quickly as one might expect at first glance. [140]

Only in 2014 did the company realize its next major redesign - this time, they went all-in with a fresh logo and design language. [141] Around this time, we can notice a significant change in the way companies have designed their solutions, focusing on flat designs with minimal elements and a greater focus on media such as images and videos. [142]

The new logo and design Airbnb introduced in 2014. Picture from Airbnb.

Re-branding in 2014 was one of the most fundamental changes, but Airbnb didn't stop there. In 2016, they redesigned their app to make it more user-friendly and intuitive for new users. [143]

In summary, we have seen how Airbnb has grown over time by focusing on UX design, which has led them from static landing pages to clean interfaces, where content pops off the screen and easy-to-navigate apps - all while staying true to what made them famous: connecting people with space to people who want to explore something new. [144]

Below you will find four takeaways from Airbnb on how they improved their conversion rates with UX over the years:

A picture is worth a thousand words

The first thing the Airbnb team learned when they went to New York and began talking to hosts was that you might not judge a book by its cover, but that it was pretty apparent that you can feel an accommodation by its photos, so this is an essential part of today's website and app.

The Airbnb team knew listings with catchy images were more popular, but they did not know how to address this discrepancy. To increase revenue, Airbnb wanted to encourage more guests to stay with them and increase the number of hosts on its platform. [145]

The difference in using a professional photographer and taking the pictures yourself can be huge! Picture from Airbnb website.

Airbnb turned to an unconventional approach. They hired a professional photographer and took high-quality photos of the residences in Airbnb's inventory. [146]

The team was surprised when they learned that the hosts were delighted with this process and joined the photographers for the shoot.

The result was positive in two ways, Airbnb says.

- Firstly, it enabled Airbnb to improve its listings with better images. As shown in the below graph, allowing photographers into homes translated into more reservations and stays. [147]

- It was also crucial for the Airbnb team to communicate with hosts. The hosts were able to make suggestions and ideas that would not have been thought of otherwise, which helped to brighten the experience for both parties.

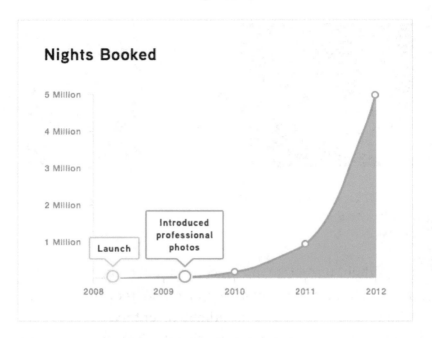

The effect of introduction of professional photos can be clearly seen as presented by Joe Zadeh during SXSW in 2012.

By using professional photographers at every location, the company learned essential lessons and immediately improved its performance. Qualified travelers are 24% more likely to book listings with high-quality photos than other listings, which has led to a 40% increase in revenue for the hosts opting for this service. [148]

Airbnb now offers professional photography services to all its hosts. Professional photographers have visited nearly 13,000 locations on six continents to ensure that each listing has detailed photos readily available for browsing and searching.

To maximize these benefits, Airbnb offers this service for free and has teamed up with more than 2,000 professionals in photography.

Airbnb knows that scale does not always lead to success, and they have proven it through minor but vital adjustments in their strategy.

A new type of referral programs

Business leaders and marketers who have been around for a while will remember how Airbnb developed a referral program that used rewards, social proof, and user data stored in email services to build one of the most successful referral programs to date. Their growth team is known for designing systems that raise awareness and lead to considerable increases in new bookings or sales. [149]

While Airbnb has shown tremendous growth over the years, its growth team constantly studies the touchpoints where it is not fully utilizing its prospects and tries to figure out how those interactions can be improved. One example is referrals. Nielsen reported 92% of consumers trusted recommendations from people they knew, so they can reach you as a new user who does not know much about what they do yet, but wants to use it - one way to get closer to you is through referrals. [150]

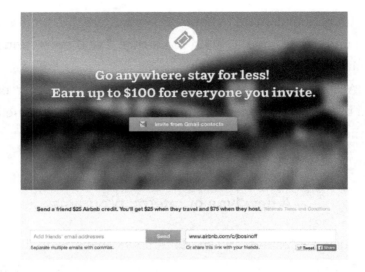

Early versions of the Airbnb referral program. Picture from Airbnb Medium.

Early in the company's history, Airbnb initiated a referral program found ineffective and largely forgotten.

"Sadly, the early version of this system wasn't something we were particularly proud of," said Growth Product Manager Gustaf Alströmer. [151]

Data gathered by the growth team indicated a positive impact on behaviors from beta testing, which went through cycles of iteration, as suggested by data, and resulted in more effective implementation.

When Airbnb interviewed other successful companies with referral programs, they found that 25-55% of their new users came from referrals.

The Airbnb team was excited about the opportunities. Jason Bosinoff, Airbnb's Director of Engineering, said in his post that

"Referrals is an exciting project because it embodies growth. It is measurable and scalable, and it all has to do with identifying a key moment for growth." [152]

The team began by looking at the data collected in the earlier version of the referral program and the companies they had spoken to. The main levers that would affect their ability to implement more effectively were:

- monthly active users sending invites
- invitees per inviter
- conversion rate to new user
- conversion rate to a new guest
- conversion rate to a new host
- and revenue potential

They sought trends or patterns from other successful companies with existing programs (25-55% of all sign-ups come through referrals). They then narrowed down what could affect these numbers:

- UX (user experience)
- CRO (conversion rate optimization)
- and business strategy.

With this information, they could start making changes that positively impact how many people turn into customers with their improved referral program.

By analyzing the "levers" they wanted to improve, Airbnb realized that each of these changes could drastically impact how practical and effective their referral program was. The potential for improvement varied from 20-90x more revenue!

Airbnb quickly discovered which methods successfully generate leads by tracking and analyzing data. This helped the company determine what to change when sending e-mails, making landing pages more compelling and suggesting improvements to listings for hosts.

The results of their analysis indicated that they could potentially add hundreds of thousands of nights booked. Curious takeaways were in the new markets, which showed higher than average booking rates when they joined the referral program.

According to their data, customers referred by other members booked more reservations with Airbnb and became hosts more often. They also sent a lot more invitations to even more users, who made the loop full circle.

The new version of the referral program produced more than 3x as many bookings as before, leading to higher revenue, membership conversions, and monthly active users sending invitations.

A better search with better data

Today's search feature of Airbnb can be used to find everything from a place to a place to explore while traveling. It can be surprising and encourage users to explore what they can offer. But it wasn't always that. Initially, it didn't know what type of data to give customers, so it decided on listings of the best quality and in a particular area based on what the user entered. [153]

As more users came to the site and Airbnb acquired more data, it could replace its basic search with a more user-data-driven search. Newman explains:

"...[W]e decided to let our community solve the problem for us. Using a rich dataset comprised of guest and host interactions, we build a model that estimated a conditional probability of booking in a location, given where the person searched. A search for 'San Francisco' would thus skew toward neighborhoods where people who also search for San Francisco typically wind up a booking, for example, the Mission District or Lower Haight." [154]

Airbnb also used data to adapt the search experience demographically. In 2014, they noticed that users from certain Asian countries typically had a high bounce rate when visiting the homepage. Analyzing the data further, they discovered that users would click on the "Neighborhood" link, start browsing photos, and never return to book a place. The data scientist who found this problem showed it to the engineering team, which created a new version of the UX design based on what users entered in the search field instead of the neighborhood list.

The search engine has evolved alongside Airbnb's need for more responsiveness and personalized results. As more users came to the site and Airbnb acquired more data as an organization, it could replace its basic search with a search based on rich data on guests' experiences at each location - just as Netflix encourages you to explore their content. The data informs the UX design, the website layout, and personalized matches.

Airbnb's brand: "Airbnb Experience."

Airbnb is about the experience. From their "Experiences" campaign to their mission statement, Airbnb's focus on providing its guests with a unique and pleasant stay has always been evident.[155]

But how did they create this?

It starts with the hosts and the way they welcome their guests into their house. Encourage them to go that extra mile by stocking the fridge with essentials, such as water and something small to eat.

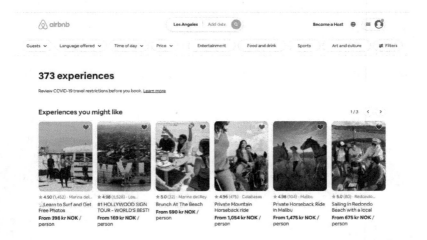

This is an example of the "Airbnb Experience." It's a critical factor in what Airbnb thinks about. And it starts with the Net Promoter Score, introduced in 2003, designed to measure customer loyalty. [156] The question raised by this metric is: How likely are you to recommend Airbnb?

The answer helps them better understand how to improve their product based on feedback from those who recommend it and minimize complaints from detractors. This data allows Airbnb to track trends for different user groups, such as women versus men, seniors, and millennials

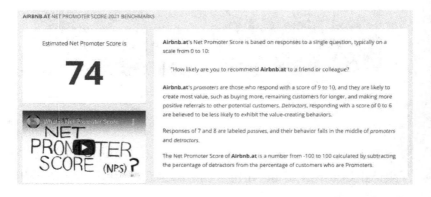

- all valuable insights when planning new products and features to their platform. [157]

Airbnb has always been committed to improving the travel experience - whether it means providing hosts with tools to manage their space and guests or connecting travelers with locals who can show them more about a city. The NPS is merely one way to measure how successful this mission is. It is also what inspires product managers like Dave Fogg and his team to brainstorm new features for Airbnb.

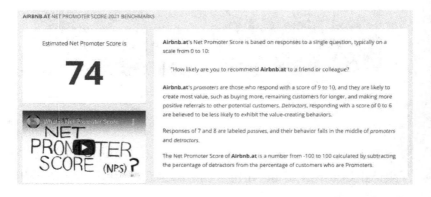

Estimated NPS score for Airbnb in 2021 by Customer Guru.

Conclusion

Airbnb is one of the world's most well-known and recognizable companies. The company has grown significantly since its inception, with over 5,6 million listings in 100,000 cities worldwide and 800 million guests staying in an Airbnb property since last year. From their detailed analyses to their understanding of human psychology in decision-making during purchase journeys or lead funnels, they have created a system that works for them in industries such as hospitality and experiences. As I mentioned earlier, there are many areas from which you can find inspiration when we look at CRO and UX at Airbnb - these are only a few!

The answer to how Airbnb has achieved such wild success could be the changes Airbnb made over ten years ago, which included changing its platform to be more user-friendly and making process changes, such as improved communication between hosts and guests.

Uber

Uber is the world's largest ride-sharing company and has been operating since 2009. The company has grown exponentially over the years and works in 10.000 cities in 71 countries worldwide. [158] In a 2018 blog post on Uber's website, it was revealed they had tested a new flow of conversion, which increased their conversion rates for their drivers in the US cities by 50%. [159] In this case study, we will deepen the business of Uber and how it will ensure that more users become passengers.

Looking at Uber today, we can see that they have created a service available to consumers to use on-demand. The company went from an experiment to a business with more than 3.9 million active drivers and operated in 10.000 cities worldwide. [160] They have built up enough brand recognition and trust to summon their services, no matter where you are or at what time of day.

The Uber app has become one of the most downloaded apps worldwide - in fact, it now has more downloads than Google Maps, and that's not even counting Uber Eats! [161] This speaks volumes about how many people have relied on this service to get from point A to point B without any other form of transport, apart from their own two feet.

The bleeding edge of technology: Use eye tracking to increase conversions

"What is eye-tracking exactly?" you may ask, and that's a good question. Simply put, it is the act of measuring and recording data on which parts of an interface people are looking at - and where they are not. This type of research has been used for years to improve everything, from how highway signs are written to what exterior car lights look like to make them more visible in driving conditions, or even something as simple as improving product packaging! Eye-tracking can be applied to everything with a screen because it helps designers understand whether their customers encounter problems interacting with their solutions and designs. [162]

Eye tracking can be done with dedicated devices like this one from TobiiPro or even eye-tracking glasses when you need to track offline behaviour. For our use, just a webcam is more than enough!

Uber has perfected the art of monetization of customer satisfaction. They are always looking for ways to improve their product, and one way they did this in 2018 was to monitor visitors on their homepage! [163] Eye movements can reveal which parts of an online experience might be more attractive than others.

The data collected in tests showed them how powerful the use of these techniques was. It provides insight into typical behavior during browsing sessions and offers potential growth opportunities within the website and landing page. Below you can see the design before and after Uber has implemented this method:

Before and after changes.

Uber has built its tools to optimize its funnels

Uber is a huge company, and only losing 1% of its users in a funnel can mean a lot of revenue is lost. They had a feeling that traditional funnel tools were not efficient enough to study their drivers and user registration experiences.

Every time they introduce changes to the UX of the app or service, the CRO team does extensive work to measure and validate them before launch, so they can understand how it will affect conversion rates. To understand how people use sign-up technology, Uber's team began a cross-functional effort to develop a new way of looking at the funnel. They call it Maze because a horn is like a maze.

When they began to build the tool, they quickly discovered they could use Maze to identify bottlenecks in the registration process. [164]

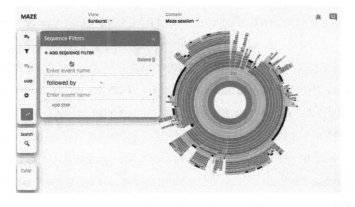

Maze in action, picture from Uber Engineering.

The Maze team is now focused on expanding it and using it for many other flows within Uber, such as rider pick-up or drop-off, customer service interactions, etc.

Building your tools, rather than relying on third parties, offers many benefits:

- One advantage is that you have control over every aspect, rather than being at the mercy of someone else's skills with their tools.

- Another benefit is better access and insight into user data than possible through a third party.

Building tools yourself is not always the answer, but realizing the value of measuring a funnel or user interaction in your product is the key. Huge tech companies invest a lot in UX design and analytics. This is because they know it pays off in the long run, users are more engaged, conversion rates increase, and revenue increases.

The Maze project at Uber aimed to contribute thoughtfully and creatively to a more significant visualization effort: Funnel Health. Users can create their funnels based on all types of events using Funnel Health, and they get valuable notifications when certain conditions occur in this visual representation - such as what measures should be taken when pick-up rates for riders' trip sessions decline or there are friction points between users after the introduction of a new app version. Connected with other platforms, such as Flow, Maze can give an in-depth insight into how each channel works for Uber.

Fine-tuning every step of the way: pickup

Uber is at the forefront of innovation in its pickup process. They made it so that drivers can verify who they are picking up and make sure it is safe to enter a stranger's car.

The verification process makes their customers feel more comfortable knowing that they are not tricked into getting into a car with someone dangerous. And now, in 2021, with mask verification, both the diver and the customer feel safer and uncomfortable during their trip.

The drop-off process is also essential. Uber has made the process seamless and quick for both parties, making it less likely that a driver will leave before being paid, or the customer leaves without paying his fare because he thought he was in an empty car.

With the pandemic verification of users in the form of masks became even more important. Photo by Charles Deluvio on Unsplash

Conclusion

Have you been searching for inspiration from Uber to increase conversion rates? If so, I recommend taking a closer look at how they optimized their funnels. They built their tools to optimize their funnels and tweak them every step of the way. This is an example of a company that has succeeded in optimizing UX and CRO. There are many companies to look for inspiration from if you want to improve your digital marketing strategy!

Shopify

Do you want to know how Shopify has increased its conversion rates and made excellent UX? Well, this case study will cover exactly that! Shopify has become the world's leading trading platform, helping retailers grow from $128 million to over $5100 billion in annual sales. [165]

We will examine how Shopify uses UX to increase conversion rates and create effective UX for its users. In addition, we will discuss improvements in CRO introduced through the combination of these two strategies.

When discussing Shopify, there are two ways to look at it:

- How they design their platform for their merchants,
- and how they create their platform for the end customer.

So let's start with UX design for merchants. Shopify takes care of domains, hosting, back-end functionality, and some front-end features, so merchants can focus their time on selling their products.

The second part is how Shopify designs its platform for end-users. The aim is to ensure that every visitor who comes across a product page or website finds relevant information about the business, which will help them decide whether they want to buy from this company.

Diversity is key

The job of a UX designer is to ensure that the user has a positive experience with your product. The task of a CRO expert is to improve these experiences and increase conversions. But what if all these designers were white men?

Telling a story, in one way, will only get you so far as it becomes repetitive. Every person in the world has different needs and desires when using a website or app, including age, gender identity, ethnicity, and more. Diversity creates better products because people with diverse backgrounds have different perspectives.

The Shopify UX design team has learned this lesson well.

"I'm a big believer that cross-functional teams with a lot of diversity of thought get us to better results," says Amy Thibodeau, Director of UX at Shopify. [166]

Shopify is an international company with users from around the world. Designing software that communicates well in all these languages and cultures can be an enormous challenge. By hiring diverse staff, they can use their design skills to communicate better with the customers they usually do not serve.

Shopify's UX Design team consists of a wide range of people from different backgrounds and cultures, helping them better understand the needs of all types of customers. [167]

Today's world offers more opportunities than ever before, so it should be our goal that everyone can strive for success while being represented in every industry or field they work in. A higher level of diversity at Shopify allows them to have an even more significant impact on this mission by including perspectives they might not otherwise think about. Diversity leads to innovation!

Diversity is illustrated in the illustrations that Shopify today uses in its systems and applications and is an integral part of its brand. Illustration from Shopify.

A holistic approach to design

A holistic approach to UX design and CRO is the only way to go if you want your customers to have a pleasant experience.

The most successful companies in the world better understand their customers than anyone else because they know what makes them tick.

Shopify has recognized this, which is why they believe a holistic approach is necessary to achieve success.

One thing all Shopify employees will tell you is they love "to get things done." To do this, they use a project cycle called GSD (Get Shit Done), which helps them stay on track with their work. [168]

The phases of the GSD define an idea and make it happen:

- Explore Possibilities and Converge on One
- Create something new for your product or service

The above approach allows Shopify's designers to align with what is happening around them while working together in UX design, research, content strategy, and front-end development. It also means fewer meetings because everyone knows their role and has clear expectations of each person contributing to the final product.

UX designers will also work with other team members, such as product managers and engineers if they need input on various aspects, such as functionality requirements or feedback on usability tests so that everyone agrees with what we are building.

Storytelling in Design: Helping users move forward

The best stories help us understand our world. They can be used to explain things we do not understand or simply entertain. [169] We will detail how Shopify uses storytelling in design to take its users on a journey from confusion to understanding and hopefully have them wanting more!

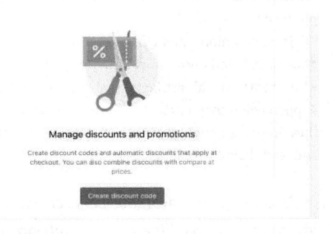

Illustrations on a platform like Shopify should be used to guide the user through the tasks that need to be done, and to tell a story about what he is currently doing.
Illustrations by Shopify Polaris Design System.

186

Communication is the most critical aspect of a design. You have to communicate with people and share ideas. Communication is what allows you to work with other people on ideas. Effective communication is when you can talk about problems, find solutions, and share your thoughts. Each team has different ways of communicating, but I have found these four foundations are always proper: good listening, interpersonal skills, practice speaking skills, and empathy for others.

When we talk about communication on a platform like Shopify, storytelling through illustrations and texts is critical, and Shopify increasingly relies on it for its platforms.

In my opinion, the main goal of design is to help people understand and move forward. Designers are storytellers who create visual artifacts that inform users what will happen when they interact with the product or service. Here they improved their style of illustrations to tell this story and lead their customers to success.

"I think people working on user experiences can use a lot of storytelling tools to onboard people and teach them how to navigate and use a digital product," says Amy Thibodeau, Director of UX at Shopify. [170]

It is not enough to have a well-designed interface. We must ensure that we design for the user and their goals, regardless of what they might be.

Why the hell would a UX designer learn to ship code?

You're a UX designer. You know you need to pay attention to details and offer an intuitive user experience, but you don't know HTML or CSS. It is time for you to learn how to code.

As a designer, you should and can learn to ship code. If you are lucky enough to work in a place like Shopify, it will be supported as you take on this new challenge.

When I work with my design processes, I work closely with my entire team, the project manager, front-end developer, back-end developer (depending on the project), and other designers. To communicate my ideas and to think about design, I find it essential to understand their field of expertise, to know what they are talking about, and how to translate my design language into something they can understand.

When I started to learn to code, it was scary and overwhelming. It seemed like an endless list of new things to know that we're so different from UX. But coding is simply another tool in my UX toolbox, not an individual field or industry, as many people believe.

Looking at Shopify, I believe that some of its success comes directly from this, as we have discovered in their holistic approach above. They have designers, UX researchers, product managers, and engineers on the same team. [171]

The other important reason is that they create a passion for design and technology - the ability to speak the language means you can impact both areas! Designers are always looking for more technical skills because they want to be better in their jobs. Yes, it's scary, but with practice, everything becomes more accessible.

Use of illustrations to communicate

If you've ever used the web (as I guess everyone reading this book has!), you know how difficult it can be to understand something from merely a static image. Shopify knows this too well and has experimented with different illustration styles for years to better communicate with its customers.

The reason Shopify decided to start a redesign of its illustration was the feedback that the pictures made it difficult for the brands of each merchant to come alive, and the immersive graphics did not do much to reconcile their brand message. [172]

To start rethinking their illustration style, Shopify's design team looked closely at how other companies design and use illustrations in their marketing material. They wanted to understand what messages these brands were trying to send with their images and a better way to communicate. They found that some brands used illustrated characters or real-life photos to represent themselves. Still, many others relied on flat graphics to make product benefits easier to understand. This led them on an unusual path, in which they began to experiment with more polished graphics with simple iconography than fully illustrated scenes.

Shopify decided to use images for a much more visual effect in its marketing and main website, but use illustrations in its actual app to create a cleaner and easier understanding of user flows when people are focused and working.
Illustration from Shopify UX Blog.

Shopify's illustration style deliberately attempted to represent who Shopify's merchants are. Most Shopify illustrations have been the author alone (whether male, female, race, etc.). Still, they decided to change their illustrators' work to use photo references for any depictions to ensure that everyone felt represented in their illustrations throughout Shopify.

They now feel confident that their new style will achieve the goals they set out to achieve. It is more apparent, conveys information literally and explicitly, and should give merchants confidence in Shopify's help in building and managing their business. As they continue to work in this new style, it will develop over time. They hope that it can be something they build on for a long time.

Conclusion

It isn't easy to find a company that does UX, CRO, and design, as well as Shopify. In this case study, we looked at how Shopify increased its conversion rates with the correct UX design principles and storytelling techniques.

It is worth looking at how Shopify has built a holistic team around its product and invested in understanding the bigger picture of its customer, and in turn, uses it to create a user experience that helps many entrepreneurs start and build an income for themselves.

7.

TIPS ON HOW TO IMPROVE YOUR WEBSITE'S CONVERSION RATES

Your website's conversion rate is one of the most critical factors in determining your success. But what are some simple things you can do to raise that number?

We have looked at several examples and methods to increase conversions, but it might be challenging to grasp how to apply these methods to your work. You might wonder what factors contribute to CRO? The answer is UX, usability, brand trustworthiness, and relevance. To ensure your investment in CRO pays off in the long run for your business, it is essential to have a step-by-step strategy that delivers results and does not require too much time or money to do it.

Some benefits of focusing on Conversion Rate Optimization and an excellent CRO strategy:

- Save time by creating high-converting content your readers want to read.
- Use your content to create a comprehensive marketing campaign that converts.
- Stop wasting time on tedious and overwhelming tasks that do not lead to conversions.
- Increase the ROI of your advertising campaigns.

In this chapter, we will dive a little deeper into the actual measures you can take at the moment to increase the conversion rate of your website.

Define the goals of the conversion rate on your landing page

How do I boost the conversion rate? Everything starts with defining measurable goals for your site before assessing visitor behavior against these defined goals. Once this is done, it becomes easier to create something that will help convert visitors across the board. [173]

When I analyze websites or a landing page, I love to ask people what their primary business goal is. Their most important business goal is usually the key to a high ranking in Google or a high conversion rate!

I ask them this question because if we do not know our goals, there is no way to evaluate a website or sales page against something specific. If you tell me your goal is "to have potential customers read about products," I am sorry, but that is not tangible. It does not provide any information on how effective a campaign is or where to focus on increasing that conversion rate. So remember – always have clear goals in mind for conversion rate optimization.

Here I have outlined some commonly accepted and achievable web page-specific conversion rates targets:

- Page sessions
- Form submissions
- Clicks through your website
- Add to cart clicks
- Sign-ups

Collect and analyze visitor data to boost the conversion rate on your website

Without data, you will not increase the conversion rate on your website. Many UX designers and marketers start with assumptions or estimates, but that is a big mistake. It is essential to constantly monitor and analyze your website data to learn more about your potential customers to better direct conversion rate optimization efforts. If you set your business goals, you also need to measure whether the company achieves the targets! [174]

The following are some key data points you want to track to understand your website visitors' behavior: [175]

- Traffic and traffic sources.
- Details of user behavior on the active landing page.
- Bounce rates for websites and form abandonment rates
- Click-through rates for advertising and digital marketing campaigns.

If you have collected quantifiable data from these areas about your existing customers, it is time to create an online persona of your ideal user. This representation contains all valuable information that will help conversion optimization campaigns be more effective and increase the conversion rate on the website, as well as test various design options for usability problems on the website. [176]

195

As an add-on to this book, I have also created a free-to-download workbook containing several tools you can use on your CRO journey. It also includes several templates for personas. You can go to radahl.no to get your free copy or buy a physical copy.

Performing competitor analysis can boost the conversion rate

You know how competitive the world is nowadays. It is essential to keep one step ahead of your competitors, including understanding what they are doing in terms of conversion rate optimization. One way to do that? Competitor analysis! Instead of simply looking at their e-commerce website for inspiration or ideas on where to improve your website's conversion rate, analyze them – analyze all aspects from UX design to marketing techniques like email marketing campaigns and what they write about in the latest blog post. This gives you a clear idea and an edge over your competitors. [177]

Here are some key points:

- Understand how your competitors do CRO to boost the conversion rate.
- Get to know their mistakes and successes.
- Find out how they do landing pages and what makes them work and not.

- Know precisely what you're faced with within the industry.
- Keep one step ahead of your competitors.

Create a sales funnel

It is best to use sales funnels if you want the customer to feel more comfortable and better understand what they are buying. This is crucial for expensive and complicated products. For example, if you have a software product, instead of asking for the sale immediately after showing your demo or free trial version, it may be more effective to offer an email course on how to use the product. This will help build trust and prove you are knowledgeable in this area.

You can also create sales funnels by creating different price tiers. For example, if you have an online knitting course and your student wants to buy the premium plan for $100/month, it might be better to offer a free trial first, then a basic package at a lower price ($25), then one with more features but less frequent access (for $500) before finally offering the premium package.

It is essential to find the balance between what you want to achieve (the conversion) and what the visitor wants. This can be done by offering free content and other valuable content on your topic, like blogs and white papers, to build trust.

The visitor will want to know that they can trust you with their money before giving it to you. They may not be interested in your product immediately, so don't pressure them or offer too much directly. Give them time and show them how valuable the content is first. Once the relationship has been established (through email drip campaigns), you can ask for the sale.

It is essential to build that trust over time, and some even say you have to contact a potential buyer six times before they are likely to buy from you.

So take your time and don't pressure the potential buyer because this can lead them away instead of purchasing. Offer value before you ask for the sale. Start by simply capturing their email address so you can continue to talk to them and bring them closer to buying something from you in the future.

Analyze your conversion funnel and find mistakes

A conversion funnel is when a user finds the product they want to buy and then decides whether to buy it. This is typically done through a series of steps, in which some users are more inclined than others to take the next step.

Although there are various types of conversion funnels, most go like this:

1. Find the product they want
2. Find out more about the product
3. Consult friends or family
4. Add to cart
5. Checkout
6. Purchase

For those with low interest in taking the next step, you can increase the conversion rate by determining what would make them more inclined to do so. Some good examples include simplifying your checkout process or giving reasons to buy now (e.g., a "limited-time offer").

When assessing your conversion funnel, it is best to identify the point at which people are likely to abandon their purchase. This can be found by analyzing data from tools like Google Analytics and Hotjar or other tracking and identifying drop-offs at each user journey stage. This will happen at the cart (due to financial commitment), so it is essential to increase your conversion rate at this stage.

An average of 69% of those who go through the checkout process will abandon their carts. [178] It is not always clear how many people who leave their carts will return, but a boost in your conversion rate, even a little, can make a huge difference. One of the easiest things to do is, for example,

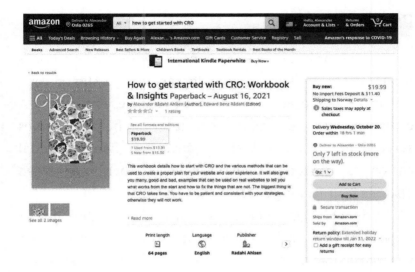

Amazon does an amazing job with their 1-Click checkout.

offer free shipping to your clients.

Amazon provides an example of how simplifying the checkout process can boost conversions: its one-click checkout systems are designed to make this part of the purchasing process easier and quicker for customers. They have figured out which steps lead to higher conversion rates and created an interface that eliminates unnecessary steps.

Create a compelling and clear value proposition

A value proposition is the one sentence that describes what a company does, who it's for, and why it should care. It's also called a promise statement or "elevator pitch." A compelling and clear value proposition can help companies succeed in marketing their products by giving potential customers a reason to choose them over other brands when opening your landing page.

In the old days, when sales happened through phone or in person, a persuasive value proposition was crucial. When you had to convince someone that your product was worth buying and not comparable alternatives from other brands, you have to articulate what makes it stand out. Your value proposition forces clarity of thought and essential facts about your brand into a concise sentence! But this applies as much today as on the phone 50 years ago for conversion optimization. If you have a value proposition for the user when they get to decision-making, it could be what convinces them to click on that buy button!

Benefits of having a clear and compelling value proposition to boost conversions:

- Communicate the benefits of your product and why it is better than competitors.

Both Mailchimp and Klaviyo offer a clear value proposition right when you land on their page, helping new users understand what they are about and improving their conversion rate.

- Tells you who your product is for – providing a short, succinct description of your customer's most pressing needs
- Remember that a value proposition is for customers and potential employees (shorter pitch for marketing to them).
- It is flexible so that it can be developed into different versions according to the quality desired.

Add a testimonial from one of your customers

You've seen them before; testimonials from happy customers are everywhere. They're on product pages, landing pages, and even blog posts. Why? Because they work!

Humans are herd animals; we tend to look for confirmation in a crowd while buying. This can get hard when you shop online. More often than not, I will hear a comment in a user testing that the customer feels "alone" while shopping online; testimonials play a big part in converting the customer to a sale.

In e-commerce, there is a fine line between creating interest and scaring away customers. To optimize your conversion rate, you need to find the optimal balance of social proof from existing customers that encourages customer conversions. Social proof can come in many forms – reviews, testimonials, endorsements, ratings, and more. Online buyers are more comfortable purchasing from a store when they realize that their friends and family have done so. Social proof is, therefore, an essential component of conversion optimization.

According to a study, 27% of customers use reviews and social proof to determine which company to support. By contrast, only 24% of consumers never consult a company's online evaluation before purchasing. [179] Customers nowadays have many options, and reviews can be an essential tool to narrow them down and increase your store's conversion rate.

If you're looking for an easy, free way to get more testimonials and sell your product or service at the same time, here are some things you can do:

- Reach out to customers on social media and ask if they would like to share their experience with your company
- Have a customer email sign up where visitors can request a quote from your business
- Ask customers who have made purchases in person what they think of it all! They may not be as shy about sharing this information right away (while walking out of the store) as someone online!

Another pro tip is setting up e-commerce tracking, which will help track how many visits come through that eventually lead to sales. Tracking these stats gives a fuller picture and can also help you ask for the testimonials at the right time.

Social proof can be a powerful tool for businesses and consumers alike, but it is essential to remember two sides. If your Facebook feed or Twitter account has negative social media posts about your product or service, you may fall victim to this phenomenon – discourage potential customers from trying out the products or services you sell.

The problem worsens with online reviews published on social channels, where every person's voice is strengthened by contacting companies directly and publicly with their concerns. This means you have to respond quickly when dealing with complaints about your products. Otherwise, it may appear you are not taking complaints seriously.

Companies can use positive social proof to their advantage. If you receive an excellent review on TrustPilot or another site, consider putting it on your site – perhaps as part of a dedicated review page or the product page. You can also consider incorporating it into your social media strategy to show your customers and reputation.

Include an image that will catch the reader's eye and draw them in

When it comes to website design, images are a vital component in creating a successful user experience. Images can be used for many purposes, such as filling space on the page, illustrating how something works, or even highlighting an action button.

One of the essential elements of e-commerce is the quality of the product page. [180] Customers are more likely to buy products if they can get a beautiful visual representation of the products you sell. Make sure the images are of high quality and be creative with how you display your products. You can use special effects or even embed video to get people excited about the product they are looking for!

Did you know that visual presentations, such as photos and videos, are the most effective way for around 65% of people to learn? [181] Visually explaining your products and showing how they can be used can hugely impact your conversion rates. Another fascinating and relevant fact is that when businesses use more exciting pictures in their marketing materials, they get up to 94% more eyeballs on their marketing content than their competitors. [182]

How can I use images to increase conversion rates for my website?

- To start, if you already use images, my first suggestion would be to add more photos. More ideas may not seem like they will increase conversion rates, but in reality, they do. If the visitor has a hard time understanding what your website is about and you have an image that captures their attention, then this increases chances of them staying on the page longer, which could lead to purchase or engagement with other content on the page (yes that includes reading long-form content).
- Images can also be used as testimonials. Mainly when someone, who came from outside of your site,

provides feedback via images of the products or even them together with your product. This is a great way to increase conversion rates because you show how it works and the benefits of your product.

- Lastly, images can be used for instructional purposes. If someone needs instructions on how something functions or an action button they need help with, then using a picture can do just that! It will not only guide them but also engage their senses in understanding what's happening, which could lead to engagement with future content as well.

Use these three techniques together, and you'll see an instant change within your website, converting more visitors into customers or leads.

It is more important to show your product in good light than it might seem. A first impression means everything when you want a person's trust, which starts with getting them to notice the branding and product photos! As soon as they realize that something looks excellent or valuable, an image or video will help ensure this continues throughout their journey by learning what kind of products you offer on your e-commerce. So go ahead: try to make yourself look fabulous (or at least like someone worth knowing)!

Keep your copy short, concise, and to the point - don't overwhelm readers with too much information

We all know that consumers are busy and time-starved. They don't have the luxury of spending hours on your website when they need to get back to work or take care of their families. On the other hand, we also know that copywriting can be a daunting task. And to create an engaging blog post, you may feel like there is no way around it - you're going to need more than five sentences in your intro paragraph!

Websites often neglect to focus on copywriting and product descriptions, but this can be expensive. Product page copies are crucial for conversion rates. They provide more detailed information about your products to help potential customers make an informed decision when purchasing from your online store! It could also give them competitive advantage by making it easier than others who do not effort into their web content strategy.

In search engines such as Google, where customer reviews play such an important role in ranking websites, it is more important than ever to provide your customers with excellent writing and informative content.

With the abundance of information, we are exposed to every day, our attention span is becoming shorter. [183]That means the majority of your visitors will bounce off your site after reading just a sentence or two. This makes it more critical than ever to keep your copy short, concise, and to the point.

A recent study by Unbounce in 2020 shows that the copy that works best for e-commerce websites is easy to read and effectively conveys the message. [184] They recommend your content be written for middle school reading. Try to make every sentence as concise and straightforward as possible to get your news.

Writing content that engages, sells, and is not too long is a real challenge for even the most seasoned writers. That's why it helps to have a few tools and tricks in your arsenal.

My five favorite copywriting tips are:

- Use short sentences - Keep paragraphs under 100 words
- Use the inverted pyramid structure for more complex topics, gradually revealing information as you go down below the surface layer. This way, people can read at their own pace and not get overwhelmed with too much information all at once!
- Be conversational
- Add quotes from experts or other industry leaders into your content if possible (with proper attribution)
- Build on what others say about you by quoting them

Make sure you have a call-to-action on every page so visitors know what they should do next

Think of it in this way: imagine walking down a sidewalk and noticing a fascinating storefront with a sign that says "free samples inside." You will probably go in to see the free goodies. Because there was a clear call-to-action on the door - get something for nothing!

Your website is no different. If someone visits your website searching for information or perhaps only explores what you offer, they should find clear instructions on contacting you or buying your product without any problems.

The website should have a visible and precise call-to-action in its sales funnel or on every product page, which will invite customers to take advantage of discounts, buy products at the moment, etc. But you also have to be careful because if your site has too many CTAs, it leads to confusion. You should carefully choose the most relevant call-to-action for each page and offer only one action per page to avoid adverse user experience.

Most users now witness a call-to-action when they go to any website or app, so users will search for them when they land on your website.

UX not only makes a website pleasant and comfortable for visitors but also ensures that there is an even better experience with clear instructions on what people should do next after visiting your website. CRO and UX have one thing in common - you have to optimize both strategies together if you want more conversions, as this can lead to higher ROI. Companies that focus exclusively on UX often fail without thinking about their customers' perspectives. It is important not only how usable something is but also how effective it is in achieving its goals, such as increasing sales or user enrollment.

It is also crucial that e-commerce companies use a distinct CTA button color because this helps visitors understand what they should do next. You also need to ensure that the CTA button of the website is always above the fold – which means it does not have to scroll down on mobile devices or longer pages.

Write about topics relevant to your target audience

You know the old saying, "You can't please everyone?" Well, it's true. It is impossible to satisfy every person who comes into contact with your brand, including your customers, prospects, partners, employees, and even the people responsible for reviewing your content before publishing it.

When you start doing the right UX research, you will get a good idea of the different people you will be catering to. This is useful when you or your content writers start writing for the project you are working on.

User experience is critical. You must never forget that you are writing for your target audience, not for yourself or the person who checks what you have written before publishing it.

You want to know who will read your content so that their attention can be focused where it needs to be most on the page - on the information they need about your product, service, or blog post.

Each paragraph should also have only one main topic of discussion. The more you can structure your content for easy reading, the better. Be aware of the use of jargon and industry-specific terms. Your audience may not know what these words exist or mean.

Some guidelines that I follow myself:

- If you write for a blog post about SEO (search engine optimization), don't think it's okay to talk about SEO methods like Panda updates without actually explaining what it's like.

- Make sure to include keywords wherever possible so that when people search for your content on Google, they can easily find your site and use it for their research or get the information they are looking for. In addition, try to place them near the beginning of sentences so that readers can identify them as quickly as possible in the text. You want viewers who scan all those results on their screens to land here!

- Finally, remember: Always remember that UX is key! For visitors to stick around after reading an article or watching a video from your site, you must ensure the UX is superb.

I hope this has helped clarify some things about writing relevant content for your target audience that affect your UX strategy, with clear examples of what to do - and not.

Lead the user to other parts of your website or app to discover more products and services

Do you want your users to explore more of what your website, e-commerce, or app has to offer? If so, it is essential that they quickly discover new content. One way is to implement internal links or searches to find content on their terms. The other method is to include an element in your design that encourages exploration.

Use of internal linking

Readers tend to click around more when they want to learn more about a topic. If you have a lot of content on your site, you should use internal links to guide them there. This will also help increase the time the reader spends on the site and reduce the bounce rate.

First, you should think about your keywords and what users might search for to find your content. Then you should take this list and create links to all this content by creating tags, labels, or other ways to group pages with similar information. It is also important not to make it too difficult for users to get around by using broad categories such as "retail" or "shopping." These are too general and could be used to connect to more significant types. Instead, you should use more specific terms, such as "men's clothing" or "women's handbags."

It would help if you also considered monitoring broken links of internal and external links. If someone is browsing your website and external links do not work, it will reflect poorly on you and your content. It is also wise to ensure that external links are opened in a new tab so that they do not leave your website. You can set external links with a target to be _blank, so it opens separately from your website. This will, of course, reduce the bounce rate, and I'm sure you can see this effect in Google Analytics.

Use of internal search to help the user and rank better in search engines

Most people have had the experience of not finding the information they are looking for on a web page, which makes visitors bounce. This is because many website owners do not optimize their sites for search. If your visitors do not find what they are looking for on your site, Google and Bing crawling bots will undoubtedly find it difficult to find your site's relevant content.

Simple steps can be taken to improve the searchability and discoverability of your website or e-commerce. Humans scan websites and digital products in a specific routine. By following this pattern, you're already on your way to creating an experience that is easy to understand for your visitors. Make sure to use clear messaging, colors with enough contrast, images, and lead the users to where you want them! And never forget to encourage your users to discover more of your content with the help of internal links between your blog post or products.

The importance of search engine traffic cannot be overstated, so much so that some companies pay more than $900 per click on Google Ads. [185] The reason traffic is so valuable is that it has a high intent, which means people who type "blue evening dress" into Google are looking for a particular product or solution to their problem. They are already in the mindset of buying or discovering a solution to their problem, and their intention is firm.

How I apply a sense of exploration to my projects

Every time I work on a new project, I make sure to map user journeys. I then use them to explore alternative ways to introduce the content on pages that encourage the exploration of more products, articles, and other content. This can often lead to up-sales, cross-sales, and other means of income for the company.

Here are some methods that I usually implement:
- A search bar on every page (or landing page) does not require a log-in or other information.

- Use of infinity scroll and internal links to related content at the bottom of the articles, which can be accessed by simply scrolling through the article's conclusion.
- Related products/services found at checkout can sell additional items, such as shipping services, etc.
- I have also used a section like "more from us" after the end of the articles, as well as other means of promoting the exploration of different types of devices.

Remember, it is crucial that users can quickly discover new content when they explore your website or app, so adding this element is vital!

An excellent example is Vogue, where every article has tons of other content to explore at the end of an article. They also ensure they link to different content throughout their articles.

Use videos to provide more information about your products or services

A video is an art form. It can be used to tell a story, create a mood, or set the tone for your company's voice. It can also show the product or service you sell from a more controlled angle and give the person viewing the video the exact feeling you want to convey. And, as we have already mentioned, 65% of people are visual learners.[186]

The video you choose should always reflect the message you want to convey to make it more memorable and effective for your target audience.

Videos can be used as a tool for storytelling or to highlight product features and benefits while connecting with your target audience. Its easy-to-read format will ensure you reach the right people who want information quickly, without having to spend a lot of time reading a lengthy text. The best part? A video has no language barriers, as it is universal in its form.

Add social media buttons that visitors can share on their networks

Whether you sell a product or simply want to get the word out, social media is an integral part of your marketing strategy. It's so vital that it can sometimes make or break what you're trying to do.

According to a recent study based on 100.000 randomly selected articles, more than 50% of them had two or fewer Facebook interactions. [187] So if you want to increase your chance of gaining new followers and customers, it's time to improve your game.

Fortunately for you, I will help! Here are four proven ways to increase social media shares that I apply to my content:

1. **Implement Share Buttons in Your Content** - To make people share your content easily, make sure they have all the necessary buttons at their fingertips. Provide Share buttons, including Facebook Likes, Twitter Tweets, and other social channels your potential customers use.

2. **Create Exclusive Content** - It's essential to keep people back for more. This means you have to provide them with fresh content only available on your site or through another channel, such as email marketing. You can do this by adding new videos, blogs, and product updates at least every few weeks.

3. **Jumpstart your social media engagement** - The best way to get followers (and subsequently share) is to start conversations with potential customers in social media forums where they are already talking about topics like yours! Post comments, ask questions and be active in these discussions. So if you share a link, everyone knows it is worth reading because YOU said that.

4. **Add photos/videos to your products and blog posts** - Nothing triggers a memory like seeing an image of something you've seen before.

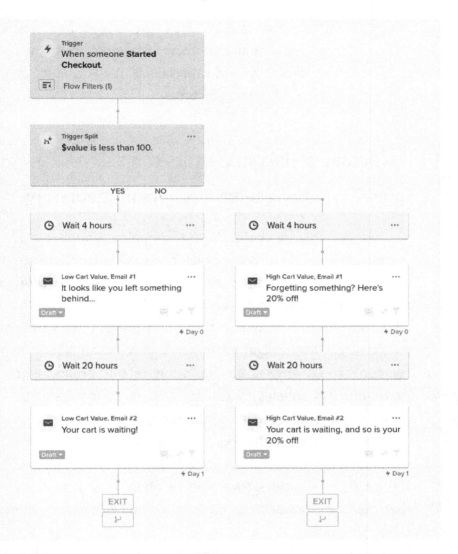

This example of cart abandonment from Klaviyo is wonderful! It segments the users into high and low value carts and sends them highly customized email reminders to convert them into paying customers.

Adding photos and videos to your website's blog posts will help customers remember what they are reading about, especially if it's a product or service with many features.

Include a chat so visitors can ask questions and receive answers immediately

Imagine this scenario: You're shopping online for a product, but you don't know which one to choose. There are many options, and you want to make the best decision possible so that your purchase is worthwhile.

Maybe there is only one thing that prevents you from purchasing - the lack of customer service at all hours. If someone could answer any questions about products or their shipping policies in real-time, it would be easier to decide which product to buy and when to place an order.

A chat can offer this type of instant customer service without having customers wait on hold or contact customer service representatives by e-mail or phone - two methods that take time away from other work and often hurt the conversion rate.

A study by eMarketer found 60% of the users asked would return to a website because they had the opportunity to chat live with sellers. They also found that 40% who used live chat services would turn to regular customers and buy more than once from a brand. [188] With this kind of insight, there is no excuse not to implement a chat service!

Chats are an excellent way to contact your customers. They allow you to get feedback and have conversations about their experiences on your website in real-time. Chat conversion rates can be increased by adding prompts that encourage customers to chat with you and by adding a FAQ section, so they know what they will find when they start chatting with you.

Follow up on abandoned carts

Abandoned carts are a perplexing problem for e-commerce websites. It is essential to monitor these abandoned cars to generate profit and create a positive customer experience.

The question is, how do you contact these shoppers? There are many ways to do this, but typically e-commerce websites have e-capture forms integrated into the checkout process so that the customer can give their e-mail address and be contacted later about their possible purchase. You can also create an incentive for shoppers to return by giving them a discount code that they can use in the future when they return to finish their transaction.

According to Baymard Institute, the average industry standard for abandoned carts is a whopping 70%! [189] This is a lot of lost customers and revenue that you can quickly recoup with some simple optimizations. If we look at it in terms of pure dollars, it's $18 billion a year lost down the drain. [190]

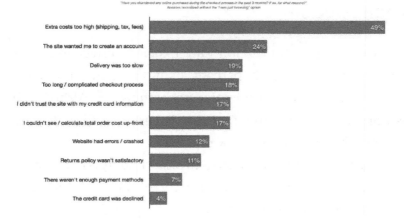

Reasons for abandonment during checkout from Baymard Institute.

When I tackle this problem, these are some things I always make sure to keep in mind:

- Make sure your checkout saves the customer e-mail as soon as they fill it in so that you can follow up with an abandoned e-mail and give them an incentive, such as a discount, to encourage them to pick up the items.
- Use targeted ads for advertising the items they have in the cart with a discount or incentive on social media and Google.
- If you personalize remarketing ads with the proper segmentation and message, you can get up to 1,300% ROI! [191]

Simplify the checkout process of your e-commerce site

According to Conversion Rate Experts, conversions may be increased by 35.62 percent using some of the most common checkout optimization techniques. [192] Although it is not easy to reach this figure, it is certainly feasible with modest changes to the check-out page.

The need to create an account was cited by 34 percent of respondents as one of the primary reasons for cart and checkout abandonment, according to Baymard Institute. [193] Already here, we have an easy fix to increase your conversion rate with the help of guest checkout. If you don't have to have the user create an account, leave it out. Or you can make a checkbox option for them if they want to create it. The best option would be to create a smooth guest checkout experience that lets more visitors flow through the checkout process without any hassles of creating an account.

The following biggest reason for not going through with a purchase is the need to fill out endless forms on the checkout page. 26% of responders to the Baymard Institute study gave this reason for not becoming one of your potential loyal customers. According to the Baymard Institute, e-commerce businesses have 23.48 form components and 14.88 form fields for new non-account consumers on average. [194] This is too many fields in a checkout process and causes friction and frustration at the checkout.

"During testing, we consistently observe that users are overwhelmed and intimidated when seeing a high amount of form fields and selections," states the Baymard Institute study.

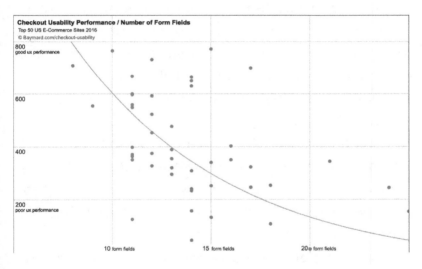

An overview of the correlation between number of form fields and UX performance. This is an excellent indicator of the e-commerce conversion rate when it comes to the checkout. Graphics from Baymard Institute.

The bar graph above shows how UX performance degrades as the number of form fields increases, and so does the conversion rate.

Some of the most optimized check processes often have half the number of fields. This is achieved by cutting out unnecessary fields and merging first and last names into one, and using live search for addresses through services such as the Google Maps API.

Attract the right website visitors

As one of the last tips I would like to mention, I would like to point out the importance of attracting the correct type of visitor. If you attract users who do not correspond to your target audience, it will not help with any of these methods because they will not be interested in what you have to offer them.

According to Jakob Nielsen, a user experience consultant with over thirty years of experience in this field, many factors play a role in the conversion rate, such as where someone comes from and their type of personality, that directly affect the conversion rate.

Jakob Nielsen prefers categorizing users into four groups:

- **Low-value referrers** – These include content aggregators that you might reach via the end of an obscure article on the internet. People who click through these recommendations are on a quest to satisfy their curiosities and aren't necessarily interested in what you're offering them. This type of

Taboola Feed

If You Spend Time on Your Computer, this Vintage Game is a Must-Have. No Install.
Forge of Empires - Free Online Game | Sponsored

The Secret Behind Babbel: An Expert Explains Why This App Is the Best for Learning a New...
Babbel | Sponsored

Here is an example of low-value referrals through Taboola's systems on CBS News.

visitor often has the highest bounce rate and lowest conversion rate.

- **Links to your website from relevant content** – These can be articles written by other authors with a genuine interest in what you offer. People who click on these links are usually the right target group and type of visitors you want. If you implement the methods in this book, you should get a high conversion rate from these kinds of visitors.

- **Search engine traffic** – I have already mentioned the value of these types of visitors in the search improvements you should make. But to sum up: these are usually highly targeted users; they could simply come to your site to get an answer to their question and nothing else. But most often, they're coming with an intention.

- **Loyal visitors** - These are people who regularly come to your website through sources such as emails and social media. They are familiar with your business as fans and subscribers, which means they are more interested in your deals than those who discover you through low-value referrals or direct links to other websites.

To increase your conversion rates, you must understand who your users and customers are. Conversion rates can be improved by attracting exemplary visitors to your website, which means understanding who they are. You can do this with the help of personas or other methods that we have talked about earlier in the book.

Conclusion

If you are struggling with your conversion rates, these tips can help. Remember that the key to a successful website is to keep things simple and focus on what matters to your target audience (ranging from price points to product features).

You need to know who your customers are and how they want to shop. You also need to ensure that the UX of your site is solid and that you follow best practices for CRO.

I know this list of methods can be comprehensive and overwhelming, so I have created a workbook to practice using these methods and better understand how to use them in real life. You can get a free copy on my website, radahl.no, or order a physical copy here.

The way forward

You're probably feeling pretty overwhelmed at the moment. With so many strategies, it is hard to know what to do for your conversion rate and what not to do. For this reason, I have put together this book on how to improve your conversions based on the basics of UX and CRO, and I want you to use it as a dictionary when you work. You should have it by your side to solve problems when you encounter an issue in UX or CRO.

Your customers want a friendly and straightforward website. They also need content that provides them with the information they are looking for as quickly as possible. This means you should not have pages on pages of text but short paragraphs that help them make a quick decision about the product or service they are interested in.

But UX and CRO require more than a few tweaks, so if you want to make it to the magical unicorn level of success, you are already on your way, as you have just finished this book that will guide you through how to approach CRO in the overall picture.

And remember, winning creates a mindset of winning. If you implement the strategies of this book, you will create a mood in which you always work with the proper methods to achieve success in the end that you pursue next.

Three key takeaways from this book:

- Engage with your target group by understanding their needs and motivations.
- Build a prototype and get user feedback early in the process.
- Find out what works or not, then refine accordingly until you have something ready to launch.

As this field is so fast-moving, it is essential to keep yourself up to date and informed about the world of UX design and CRO. If you want to get ahead of the game and learn how to apply these two areas in a way that is valuable to your business or want to know more about what CRO entails and some best practices for implementing it in UX design, I suggest you check out my blog for further reading, as it is updated almost weekly with new content.

And I would like to end with a huge thank you for buying and reading this book to the end. I hope you have found it helpful and that it has given you critical insights into how these two areas work together for business success! I will update my blog weekly with new posts on UX Design and CRO, so please subscribe if you are interested.

Sources

[1] Ian Robertson : Trinity Research - Trinity College Dublin. (2021). Retrieved 20 October 2021, from https://www.tcd.ie/research/profiles/?profile=iroberts

[2] Saleh, Khalid; Shukairy, Ayat (Nov 1, 2010). Conversion Optimization: The Art and Science of Converting Prospects to Customers. Sebastopol, California: O'Reilly Media. p. 2. ISBN 9781449397692. OCLC 733752533. Retrieved May 7, 2021.

[3] What is Conversion Rate Optimization (CRO)? The Hotjar Guide. (2021). Retrieved 10 September 2021, from https://www.hotjar.com/conversion-rate-optimization/

[4] Conversion Rate Optimization [2021 CRO]. (2021). Retrieved 10 September 2021, from https://moz.com/learn/seo/conversion-rate-optimization

[5] Google. "Google Analytics." Google Analytics, 2021, https://analytics.google.com/. Accessed 12 July 2021.

6 "Ark bokhandel." Novicell, 2021, https://www.novicell.no/vaare-kunder/ark/. Accessed 12 July 2021.

[7] Bainbridge, L. (2015). Map Out a 300% Conversion Rate Increase. Retrieved 10 September 2021, from https://conversionsciences.com/map-out-a-300-conversion-rate-increase/

8 Widerfunnel. "The Sims 3 identifies the most compelling offer to drive registrations." Widerfunnel, 2013, https://portfolio.radahl.no/sims-cro. Accessed 12 July 2021.

9 Petrovic, Jan. "How Intuit Increased Conversion Rate by 211% Just By Using Proactive Chat." Proimpact7, 9 August 2010, https://portfolio.radahl.no/proimpact7. Accessed 12 July 2021.

10 "Crazy Egg Explainer Video Case Study." Demo Duck, 2013, https://portfolio.radahl.no/crazyegg. Accessed 12 July 2021.

11 vwo. "How AMD Used VWO To Increase Social Shares By 3600%." vwo, 2015, https://vwo.com/success-stories/amd/. Accessed 12 July 2021.

[12] U.S. online shopping conversion rate 2020 | Statista. (2021). Retrieved 10 September 2021, from https://www.statista.com/statistics/439558/us-online-shopper-conversion-rate/

[13] Ecommerce Market Data and Ecommerce Benchmarks for the Fashion Clothing & Accessories Market for June 2021 . (2021). Retrieved 19 July 2021, from https://www.irpcommerce.com/en/gb/ecommercemarketdata.aspx?Market=3

[14] 12 Ecommerce Conversion Rate Statistics (Updated 2021). (2021). Retrieved 19 July 2021, from https://portfolio.radahl.no/growcode

[15] Global online shopping: device conversion rate 2020 | Statista. (2021). Retrieved 10 September 2021, from https://www.statista.com/statistics/304280/global-online-shopper-conversion-rate-by-platform/

[16] Global online shopping: device conversion rate 2020 | Statista. (2021). Retrieved 10 September 2021, from https://www.statista.com/statistics/304280/global-online-shopper-conversion-rate-by-platform/

[17] Google Analytics Usage Statistics. (2021). Retrieved 19 July 2021, from https://trends.builtwith.com/analytics/Google-Analytics

[18] Google Search Console. (2021). Retrieved 10 September 2021, from https://search.google.com/search-console/about

[19] About - Heap. (2021). Retrieved 10 September 2021, from https://heap.io/about

[20] About Us - Hotjar. (2021). Retrieved 10 September 2021, from https://www.hotjar.com/about-us/

[21] Hotjar Features - Connect All The Dots With One Powerful Solution. (2021). Retrieved 10 September 2021, from https://www.hotjar.com/tour/#recordings

[22] About Us | GTmetrix. (2021). Retrieved 10 September 2021, from https://gtmetrix.com/about.html

[23] "How website performance affects conversion rates | Cloudflare." https://www.cloudflare.com/learning/performance/more/website-performance-conversion-rates/. Accessed 12 Jul. 2021.

[24] Website, A/B Testing & Personalisation Solutions – Google Optimize. (2021). Retrieved 10 September 2021, from https://marketingplatform.google.com/about/optimize

[25] About Optimizely. (2019). Retrieved 10 September 2021, from https://www.optimizely.com/company/

[26] User Experience Optimization: Process & Methods | CleverTap. (2021). Retrieved 10 September 2021, from https://clevertap.com/blog/user-experience-optimization-process/

[27] Stewart, M. (2021). The CTA Debate: Above or Below the Fold?. Retrieved 10 September 2021, from https://www.thecreativemomentum.com/blog/the-cta-debate-above-or-below-the-fold

[28] Law, E., van Schaik, P., & Roto, V. (2014). Attitudes towards user experience (UX) measurement. *International Journal Of Human-Computer Studies*, *72*(6), 526-541. doi: 10.1016/j.ijhcs.2013.09.006

[29] E. K. Strong, Jr. The Psychology of Selling and Advertising. New York 1925, p. 349 and p. 9.

[30] Young, S. (2014). Improving Library User Experience with A/B Testing: Principles and Process. *Weave: Journal Of Library User Experience*, *1*(1). doi: 10.3998/weave.12535642.0001.101

[31] How to CRO your Product through A/B Testing in 6 keywords. (2019). Retrieved 10 September 2021, from https://blog.prototypr.io/how-to-cro-your-product-through-a-b-testing-in-6-keywords-734987887ca8

[32] Young, S. (2014). Improving Library User Experience with A/B Testing: Principles and Process. *Weave: Journal Of Library User Experience*, *1*(1). doi: 10.3998/weave.12535642.0001.101

[33] George Kingsley Zipf (1949), Human behavior and the principle of least effort, Addison-Wesley Press

[34] Principle of Consistency and Standards in User Interface Design. (2021). Retrieved 12 September 2021, from https://www.interaction-design.org/literature/article/principle-of-consistency-and-standards-in-user-interface-design

[35] Sanders, W. R. (2001). *Cognitive psychology principles for digital systems training*. US Army Research Institute for the Behavioral and Social Sciences.

[36] The Psychologist's View of UX Design | UX Magazine. (2021). Retrieved 19 July 2021, from https://uxmag.com/articles/the-psychologists-view-of-ux-design

[37] Hunt, R. (1995). The subtlety of distinctiveness: What von Restorff really did. *Psychonomic Bulletin & Review*, *2*(1), 105-112. doi: 10.3758/bf03214414

[38] Parker, A., Wilding, E., & Akerman, C. (1998). The von Restorff Effect in Visual Object Recognition Memory in Humans and Monkeys: The Role of Frontal/Perirhinal Interaction. *Journal Of Cognitive Neuroscience*, *10*(6), 691-703. doi: 10.1162/089892998563103

[39] Yablonski, J. (2021). Von Restorff Effect | Laws of UX. Retrieved 12 September 2021, from https://lawsofux.com/von-restorff-effect/

[40] Jost, T., Ouerhani, N., Von Wartburg, R., Müri, R., & Hügli, H. (2005). Assessing the contribution of color in visual attention. *Computer Vision and Image Understanding*, *100*(1-2), 107-123.

[41] Young, S. (2010). Cognitive user interfaces. *IEEE Signal Processing Magazine*, *27*(3), 128-140.

[42] Solso, R. L., MacLin, M. K., & MacLin, O. H. (2005). *Cognitive psychology*. Pearson Education New Zealand.

[43] (2021). Retrieved 19 July 2021, from https://www.reddit.com/r/apple/comments/8gz7hy/the_apple_music_app_is_horribly_designed/

[44] Typography Terms Cheat Sheet. (2021). Retrieved 12 September 2021, from https://www.nngroup.com/articles/typography-terms-ux/

[45] Xue, H., & Almeida, P. C. (2011). Nostalgia and Its Value to Design Strategy: Some Fundamental Considerations. In *Proceedings of Tsinghua-DMI International Design Management Symposium 2011*.

[46] Gross, A., & Thüring, M. (2013, January). Encountering the Unexpected: Influencing User Experience through Surprise. In *UMAP Workshops*.

[47] Landauer, T. K.; Nachbar, D. W. (1985). "Selection from alphabetic and numeric menu trees using a touch screen". Proceedings of the SIGCHI conference on Human factors in computing systems - CHI '85. p. 73. doi:10.1145/317456.317470. ISBN 978-0897911498.

[48] Hick's Law: Making the choice easier for users. (2020). Retrieved 19 July 2021, from https://www.interaction-design.org/literature/article/hick-s-law-making-the-choice-easier-for-users

[49] Cascaes Cardoso, M. (2017, May). The onboarding effect: Leveraging user engagement and retention in crowdsourcing platforms. In *Proceedings of the 2017 CHI Conference Extended Abstracts on Human Factors in Computing Systems* (pp. 263-267).

[50] Yang, F., & Shen, F. (2019). Involvement without knowledge gain: A meta-analysis of the cognitive effects of website interactivity. *Journal of Broadcasting & Electronic Media*, *63*(2), 211-230.

[51] Dake, D. M. (1993). Visual Thinking Skills for the Digital Age.

[52] Proctor, R. W., & Schneider, D. W. (2018). Hick's law for choice reaction time: A review. *Quarterly Journal of Experimental Psychology*, *71*(6), 1281-1299.

[53] Coleman, Andrew (2006). Dictionary of Psychology (Second Edition). Oxford University Press. p. 688.

[54] Tsarenko, K. (2019). UX due to the current potential users requirements and the ways to increase their number. In *The Youth of the 21st Century: Education, Science, Innovations* (pp. 274-276).

[55] Memory; a contribution to experimental psychology : Ebbinghaus, Hermann, 1850-1909 : Free Download, Borrow, and Streaming : Internet Archive. (2021). Retrieved 29 September 2021, from https://archive.org/details/memorycontributi00ebbiuoft

[56] (2021). Retrieved 19 July 2021, from https://mslindstrom.files.wordpress.com/2011/01/key_study_-_glanzer__cunitz__1966_-_serial_position_effect.pdf

[57] Glenberg, A.M; M.M. Bradley; J.A. Stevenson; T.A. Kraus; M.J. Tkachuk; A.L. Gretz (1980). "A two-process account of long-term serial position effects". Journal of Experimental Psychology: Human Learning and Memory. 6 (4): 355–369. doi:10.1037/0278-7393.6.4.355.

[58] Bjork & Whitten (1974). Recency sensitive retrieval processes in long-term free recall, Cognitive Psychology, 6, 173–189.

[59] Baddeley, A.D. & Hitch, Graham & Allen, Richard. (2009). Working memory and binding in sentence recall. Journal of Memory and Language. 61. 438-456. 10.1016/j.jml.2009.05.004.

[60] Rundus, D (1971). "An analysis of rehearsal processes in free recall". Journal of Experimental Psychology. 89: 63–77. doi:10.1037/h0031185

[61] Costabile, Kristi & Klein, Stanley. (2005). Finishing Strong: Recency Effects in Juror Judgments. Basic and Applied Social Psychology. 27. 47-58. 10.1207/s15324834basp2701_5.

[62] Serial Position Effect: How to Create Better User Interfaces. (2020). Retrieved 29 September 2021, from https://www.interaction-design.org/literature/article/serial-position-effect-how-to-create-better-user-interfaces

[63] Rådahl, A. (2021). The Five Principles of UX Design Psychology: Can You Predict the Behavior of Your Users? - RÅDAHL. Retrieved 10 September 2021, from https://radahl.no/the-five-principles-of-ux-design-psychology-can-you-predict-the-behavior-of-your-users-913784c1d66/

[64] Marcus, A., Chiou, M., Narula, C., & Yu, A. (2013, July). The innovation machine: mobile UX design combining information and persuasion design to change behavior. In *International Conference of Design, User Experience, and Usability* (pp. 67-76). Springer, Berlin, Heidelberg.

[65] Memory Recognition and Recall in User Interfaces. (2021). Retrieved 10 September 2021, from https://www.nngroup.com/articles/recognition-and-recall/

[66] Scarcity Principle in UI Design: Making Users Click RIGHT NOW or Lose Out. (2021). Retrieved 10 September 2021, from https://www.nngroup.com/articles/scarcity-principle-ux/

[67] Social Proof in the User Experience. (2021). Retrieved 10 September 2021, from https://www.nngroup.com/articles/social-proof-ux/

[68] Bowman, J. (2020). The Psychology of User Decisions. Retrieved 10 September 2021, from https://uxtools.co/blog/the-psychology-of-user-decisions/

[69] UX strategies to guide users through a complicated journey. (2018). Retrieved 10 September 2021, from https://uxdesign.cc/ux-strategies-to-guide-users-through-a-complicated-journey-6b945b61eadd

[70] Van Grinsven, B., & Das, E. (2016). Logo design in marketing communications: Brand logo complexity moderates exposure effects on brand recognition and brand attitude. *Journal of marketing communications*, 22(3), 256-270.

[71] What is Persuasive Design?. (2021). Retrieved 10 September 2021, from https://www.interaction-design.org/literature/topics/persuasive-design

[72] Willcock, D. I. (2016). Collaborating for results: Silo working and relationships that work. Routledge.

[73] Akhter, R. (2018). Impact of copywriting in marketing communication.

6

[74] Odden, L. (2012). Optimize: How to attract and engage more customers by integrating SEO, social media, and content marketing. John Wiley & Sons.

[75] Maslen, A. (2015). Persuasive copywriting: Using psychology to engage, influence and sell. Kogan Page Publishers.

[76] Weaver, B. (2019). PAS copywriting formula made even more effective. Retrieved 30 September 2021, from https://copywritematters.com/paso-copywriting-formula/

[77] Use the AIDA Formula for Writing Great Content. (2021). Retrieved 30 September 2021, from http://www.nonprofitcopywriter.com/AIDA-formula.html

[78] Weaver, B. (2019). PAS copywriting formula made even more effective. Retrieved 30 September 2021, from https://copywritematters.com/paso-copywriting-formula/

[79] Use the AIDA Formula for Writing Great Content. (2021). Retrieved 30 September 2021, from http://www.nonprofitcopywriter.com/AIDA-formula.html

[80] Eisenberg, B., CALL TO ACTION: Secret Formulas to Improve Online Results, Nashville, Tennessee, Thomas Nelson, 2006, p. 20

[81] Hernandez, A., & Resnick, M. L. (2013, September). Placement of call to action buttons for higher website conversion and acquisition: An eye tracking study. In *Proceedings of the Human Factors and Ergonomics Society Annual Meeting* (Vol. 57, No. 1, pp. 1042-1046). Sage CA: Los Angeles, CA: SAGE Publications.

[82] Cebi, S. (2013). Determining importance degrees of website design parameters based on interactions and types of websites. *Decision Support Systems*, *54*(2), 1030-1043.

[83] Bojko, A. (2013). Eye tracking the user experience: A practical guide to research. Rosenfeld Media.

[84] Almeida, F., & Monteiro, J. (2017). The Role of Responsive Design in Web Development. *Webology*, *14*(2).

[85] Mobile percentage of website traffic 2021 | Statista. (2021). Retrieved 1 October 2021, from https://www.statista.com/statistics/277125/share-of-website-traffic-coming-from-mobile-devices/

[86] Nearly 70% of Consumers Say Page Speed Impacts Their Purchasing Decisions. (2019). Retrieved 1 October 2021, from https://www.searchenginejournal.com/nearly-70-of-consumers-say-page-speed-impacts-their-purchasing-decisions/290235/#close

[87] Huijsmans, I., Ma, I., Micheli, L., Civai, C., Stallen, M., & Sanfey, A. G. (2019). A scarcity mindset alters neural processing underlying consumer decision making. *Proceedings of the National Academy of Sciences, 116*(24), 11699-11704.

[88] (2021). Retrieved 1 October 2021, from http://www.e-tailing.com/content/wp-content/uploads/2009/12/winbuyer_102209_brief.pdf

[89] Huang, W. H., Shen, G. C., & Liang, C. L. (2019). The effect of threshold free shipping policies on online shoppers' willingness to pay for shipping. *Journal of Retailing and Consumer Services, 48*, 105-112.

[90] Woodside, A. G., & Delozier, M. W. (1976). Effects of word of mouth advertising on consumer risk taking. *Journal of advertising, 5*(4), 12-19.

[91] Roethke, K., Klumpe, J., Adam, M., & Benlian, A. (2020). Social influence tactics in e-commerce onboarding: The role of social proof and reciprocity in affecting user registrations. *Decision Support Systems, 131*, 113268.

[92] Anderson, M., & Anderson, M. (2012). Study: 72% Of Consumers Trust Online Reviews As Much As Personal Recommendations. Retrieved 7 October 2021, from https://searchengineland.com/study-72-of-consumers-trust-online-reviews-as-much-as-personal-recommendations-114152

[93] Cazañas-Gordón, Alex & Miguel, Andre & Parra Mora, Esther. (2017). Estimating Sample Size for Usability Testing. ENFOQUE UTE. 8. 172-185. 10.29019/enfoqueute.v8n1.126.

[94] Liikkanen, L. A., Kilpiö, H., Svan, L., & Hiltunen, M. (2014, October). Lean UX: the next generation of user-centered agile development?. In *Proceedings of the 8th nordic conference on human-computer interaction: Fun, fast, foundational* (pp. 1095-1100).

[95] Siroker, D., & Koomen, P. (2013). A/B testing: The most powerful way to turn clicks into customers. John Wiley & Sons.

[96] Liu, F. (2008, November). Usability evaluation on websites. In 2008 9th international conference on computer-aided industrial design and conceptual design (pp. 141-144). IEEE.

[97] Barnes, B. (2018). What is the real definition of a Market Insight in the innovation world?. Retrieved 15 October 2021, from https://www.umi.us/blog/market-insight-definition/

[98] Park, J. H., Lee, S. H., Lim, G. J., Yeo, U. Y., & Kim, J. W. (2020). Multi-Dimensional Analysis Method of Product Reviews for Market Insight. *Journal of Intelligence and Information Systems*, *26*(2), 57-78.

[99] Smith, B. D., & Raspin, P. (2011). Creating market insight: How firms create value from market understanding. John Wiley & Sons.

[100] Romano Bergstrom, J. C., Olmsted-Hawala, E. L., Chen, J. M., & Murphy, E. D. (2011). Conducting iterative usability testing on a web site: challenges and benefits. *Journal of Usability Studies*, *7*(1), 9-30.

[101] Why You Only Need to Test with 5 Users. (2021). Retrieved 15 October 2021, from https://www.nngroup.com/articles/why-you-only-need-to-test-with-5-users/

[102] Results of the 2020 User Testing Industry Report. (2021). Retrieved 15 October 2021, from https://www.userfountain.com/results-of-the-2020-user-testing-industry-report

[103] Warfel, T. Z. (2009). Prototyping: a practitioner's guide. Rosenfeld media.

[104] Snyder, C. (2003). Paper prototyping: The fast and easy way to design and refine user interfaces. Morgan Kaufmann.

[105] Ficzere, P., Borbás, L., & Török, Á. (2013). Economical investigation of rapid prototyping. *International Journal For Traffic And Transport Engineering*, *3*(3), 344-350.

[106] What is User Testing? - Learn UX. (2016). Retrieved 16 October 2021, from https://www.keepitusable.com/blog/what-is-user-testing/

[107] Wilson, C. (2013). Interview techniques for UX practitioners: A user-centered design method. Newnes.

[108] Eysenbach, G. (2005). Using the internet for surveys and research. In *Evaluating the organizational impact of healthcare information systems* (pp. 129-143). Springer, New York, NY.

[109] Rabiee, F. (2004). Focus-group interview and data analysis. *Proceedings of the nutrition society*, *63*(4), 655-660.

[110] Raven, M. E., & Flanders, A. (1996). Using contextual inquiry to learn about your audiences. *ACM SIGDOC Asterisk Journal of Computer Documentation*, *20*(1), 1-13.

[111] Harper, C., Harper, C., Meingast, M., Edwards, R. E., Greene, M., Valdez, T. D., & Sidhu Maguire, A. (2020, December). How to Maximize Success in Industry as a UX Researcher. In *Proceedings of the Human Factors and Ergonomics Society Annual Meeting* (Vol. 64, No. 1, pp. 589-592). Sage CA: Los Angeles, CA: SAGE Publications.

[112] Convertino, G., & Frishberg, N. (2017). Why agile teams fail without UX research. *Communications of the ACM, 60*(9), 35-37.

[113] Høffding, S., & Martiny, K. (2016). Framing a phenomenological interview: what, why and how. *Phenomenology and the Cognitive Sciences, 15*(4), 539-564.

[114] Leech, B. L. (2002). Asking questions: Techniques for semistructured interviews. *PS: Political Science & Politics, 35*(4), 665-668.

[115] Mehrabian, A. (1969). Significance of posture and position in the communication of attitude and status relationships. *Psychological bulletin, 71*(5), 359.

[116] Müller, C., Cienki, A., Fricke, E., Ladewig, S. H., McNeill, D., & Tessendorf, S. (2013). Body-language-communication. *An international handbook on multimodality in human interaction, 1*(1), 131-232.

[117] Reja, U., Manfreda, K. L., Hlebec, V., & Vehovar, V. (2003). Open-ended vs. close-ended questions in web questionnaires. *Developments in applied statistics, 19*(1), 159-177.

[118] Burnett, J. R., Fan, C., Motowidlo, S. J., & Degroot, T. (1998). Interview notes and validity. *Personnel Psychology, 51*(2), 375-396.

[119] Parkinson, D. D. (2001). Securing trustworthy data from an interview situation with young children: Six integrated interview strategies. *Child Study Journal, 31*(3), 137-157.

[120] Jenkins, R. (2012). What to ask—and not to ask—in your interview. *Chronicle of Higher Education, 58*(25), n25.

[121] What is Design Thinking?. (2021). Retrieved 15 October 2021, from https://www.interaction-design.org/literature/topics/design-thinking

[122] Urban Dictionary: measure twice, cut once. (2021). Retrieved 16 October 2021, from https://www.urbandictionary.com/define.php?term=measure%20twice%2C%20cut%20once

[123] content: MarketingSherpa, M. (2021). Email Marketing: 208% higher conversion rate for targeted emails over batch-and-blast. Retrieved 17 October 2021, from https://www.marketingsherpa.com/article/case-study/208-higher-conversion-rate-targeted

[124] MacKenzie, I., Meyer, C., & Noble, S. (2013). How retailers can keep up with consumers. McKinsey & Company. Retrieved 17 October 2021, from https://www.mckinsey.com/industries/retail/our-insights/how-retailers-can-keep-up-with-consumers

[125] U.S. Amazon market share 2021 | Statista. (2021). Retrieved 17 October 2021, from https://www.statista.com/statistics/788109/amazon-retail-market-share-usa/

[126] Remarketing: the Ultimate Guide for 2020 - GrowthBadger. (2019). Retrieved 17 October 2021, from https://growthbadger.com/remarketing/#chapter-6

[127] 44 Cart Abandonment Rate Statistics - Cart & Checkout - Baymard Institute. (2021). Retrieved 17 October 2021, from https://baymard.com/lists/cart-abandonment-rate

[128] Fox, M. (2015). Shopping Cart Abandonment: An $18 Billion Opportunity [New Ebook]. Retrieved 17 October 2021, from https://www.dynamicyield.com/blog/shopping-cart-abandonment-ebook-announcement/

[129] Report: 2020 online shopping habits and retailer strategies. (2020). Retrieved 17 October 2021, from https://www.optimizely.com/insights/reimagining-commerce-report/

[130] Should You Ask For a Phone Number on Your Forms?. (2015). Retrieved 17 October 2021, from https://vtldesign.com/web-strategy/conversion-rate-optimization/phone-number-form-field-case-study/

[131] Taylor, M. (2016). Why Multi-Step Lead Forms Get up to 300% More Conversions. Retrieved 17 October 2021, from https://www.ventureharbour.com/multi-step-lead-forms-get-300-conversions/

[132] After "sad" Snapchat redesign, Snap loses one-fifth its value. (2018). Retrieved 17 October 2021, from https://www.cbsnews.com/news/after-sad-snapchat-redesign-snap-loses-one-fifth-its-value/

[133] Viswanathan, V., & Linsey, J. (2020). Designing with examples: a study on the role of familiarity, warnings and physical modelling. *Journal of Engineering Design*, 31(11-12), 552-573.

[134] Weber's Law of Just Noticeable Difference. (2021). Retrieved 17 October 2021, from http://apps.usd.edu/coglab/WebersLaw.html

[135] UX Research: 5 Requirements for the 'Ratings Distribution Summary' on the Product Page (65% Get it Wrong). (2021). Retrieved 17 October 2021, from https://baymard.com/blog/user-ratings-distribution-summary

[136] Local Consumer Review Survey: How Customer Reviews Affect Behavior. (2020). Retrieved 17 October 2021, from https://www.brightlocal.com/research/local-consumer-review-survey/

[137] Allow Users to Upload Images with Their Review (34% of Sites Don't). (2021). Retrieved 17 October 2021, from https://baymard.com/blog/allow-reviewers-to-upload-images

[138] About Airbnb. Airbnb. (2021). Retrieved 17 October 2021, from https://news.airbnb.com/about-us/

[139] New License to Explore: Airbnb's Nathan Blecharczyk '05. (2021). Retrieved 17 October 2021, from https://alumni.harvard.edu/community/stories/airbnb-nathan-blecharczyk-05

[140] Airbnb redesign includes Ashton Kutcher's vacation wish list. (2012). Retrieved 17 October 2021, from https://www.cbsnews.com/news/airbnb-redesign-includes-ashton-kutchers-vacation-wish-list/

[141] TechCrunch is now a part of Verizon Media. (2021). Retrieved 17 October 2021, from https://techcrunch.com/2014/07/16/airbnb-redesign/

[142] Cass, J. (2021). The Hottest Web Design Trends of 2014: Updated. Retrieved 17 October 2021, from https://justcreative.com/hottest-web-design-trends-2014/

[143] Nast, C. (2016). Good News: Airbnb's App Is Now Significantly Less Infuriating. Retrieved 17 October 2021, from https://www.wired.com/2016/04/airbnbs-new-app-overhauls-user-experience/

[144] UX Timeline, back to the past!. (2021). Retrieved 17 October 2021, from http://uxtimeline.com/airbnb.html

[145] Airbnb's Small Army Of Photographers Are Making You (And Them) Look Good. (2011). Retrieved 17 October 2021, from https://www.fastcompany.com/1786980/airbnbs-small-army-photographers-are-making-you-and-them-look-good

[146] Airbnb Photography. Airbnb. (2021). Retrieved 17 October 2021, from https://www.airbnb.no/d/pro-photography

[147] Joe Zadeh, Airbnb presentation at Lean Startup SXSW, Austin. (2021). Retrieved 17 October 2021, from https://www.slideshare.net/500startups/joe-zadeh-airbnb-presentation-at-lean-startup-sxsw-austin

[148] Airbnb Photography. Airbnb. (2021). Retrieved 17 October 2021, from https://www.airbnb.no/d/pro-photography

[149] (2021). Retrieved 17 October 2021, from https://www.youtube.com/watch?v=SS9wGKuGVt4

[150] Reports and Insights | Global Trust in Advertising and Brand Messages | Nielsen. (2012). Retrieved 17 October 2021, from https://www.nielsen.com/us/en/insights/report/2012/global-trust-in-advertising-and-brand-messages-2/

[151] Gustaf Alstromer. Crunchbase. (2021). Retrieved 17 October 2021, from https://www.crunchbase.com/person/gustaf-alstromer

[152] Hacking Word-of-Mouth: Making Referrals Work for Airbnb. (2016). Retrieved 17 October 2021, from https://medium.com/airbnb-engineering/hacking-word-of-mouth-making-referrals-work-for-airbnb-46468e7790a6

[153] Airbnb's website is one of the worst I've encountered. Airbnb Community Center. (2016). Retrieved 17 October 2021, from https://community.withairbnb.com/t5/Hosting/Airbnb-s-website-is-one-of-the-worst-I-ve-encountered/td-p/88536

[154] Location Relevance at Airbnb. (2016). Retrieved 17 October 2021, from https://medium.com/airbnb-engineering/location-relevance-at-airbnb-12c004247b07#.vtj3t52mm

[155] Ogweng, S. (2018). How Airbnb's 'Experiences' Campaign Took Over Instagram. Business 2 Community. Retrieved 17 October 2021, from https://www.business2community.com/instagram/how-airbnbs-experiences-campaign-took-over-instagram-02131974

[156] The One Number You Need to Grow. (2003). Retrieved 17 October 2021, from https://hbr.org/2003/12/the-one-number-you-need-to-grow

[157] How well does NPS predict rebooking?. (2016). Retrieved 17 October 2021, from https://medium.com/airbnb-engineering/how-well-does-nps-predict-rebooking-9c84641a79a7

[158] Uber Technologies, Inc. - Investor Relations | Uber . (2021). Retrieved 18 October 2021, from https://investor.uber.com/home/default.aspx

[159] Luo, Y., & Cukier, J. (2018). Maximizing Process Performance with Maze, Uber's Funnel Visualization Platform. Retrieved 18 October 2021, from https://eng.uber.com/maze/

[160] How Many Uber Drivers Are There In 2021? | Ridester.com. (2021). Retrieved 18 October 2021, from https://www.ridester.com/how-many-uber-drivers-are-there/

[161] Most Popular Apps (2021). (2021). Retrieved 18 October 2021, from https://www.businessofapps.com/data/most-popular-apps/

[162] Holmqvist, K., Nyström, M., Andersson, R., Dewhurst, R., Jarodzka, H., & Van de Weijer, J. (2011). *Eye tracking: A comprehensive guide to methods and measures*. OUP Oxford.

[163] How UBER optimized their home page design for conversion — eye-tracking insights. (2019). Retrieved 18 October 2021, from https://uxplanet.org/how-uber-changed-its-main-page-to-optimize-conversion-investigated-with-eye-tracking-tool-e4241b347e3d

[164] Luo, Y., & Cukier, J. (2018). Maximizing Process Performance with Maze, Uber's Funnel Visualization Platform. Retrieved 18 October 2021, from https://eng.uber.com/maze/

[165] Shopify Statistics 2021: UPDATED Facts, Market Share & More - Acquire Convert. (2019). Retrieved 19 October 2021, from https://acquireconvert.com/shopify-statistics/

[166] Designers Spilling Tea: Amy Thibodeau, Director of UX at Shopify. (2019). Retrieved 19 October 2021, from https://marvelapp.com/blog/interview-amy-thibodeau-director-ux-shopify/

[167] You can't hust Draw Purple People and Call it Diversity. (2021). Retrieved 19 October 2021, from https://ux.shopify.com/you-cant-just-draw-purple-people-and-call-it-diversity-e2aa30f0c0e8

[168] Shopify - How we Get Shit Done. (2021). Retrieved 19 October 2021, from https://vimeo.com/456735890

[169] Quesenbery, W., & Brooks, K. (2010). Storytelling for user experience: Crafting stories for better design. Rosenfeld Media.

[170] Designers Spilling Tea: Amy Thibodeau, Director of UX at Shopify. (2019). Retrieved 19 October 2021, from https://marvelapp.com/blog/interview-amy-thibodeau-director-ux-shopify/

[171] Why learning to ship code really matters for designers. (2021). Retrieved 19 October 2021, from https://ux.shopify.com/anyone-can-ship-35b9f9142c5

[172] Redesigning the illustration style at Shopify. (2021). Retrieved 19 October 2021, from https://ux.shopify.com/redesigning-the-illustration-style-at-shopify-a94dc893cd77

[173] Crossley, C. D., Cooper, C. D., & Wernsing, T. S. (2013). Making things happen through challenging goals: Leader proactivity, trust, and business-unit performance. *Journal of Applied Psychology, 98*(3), 540.

[174] Phillips, J. (2016). Ecommerce analytics: analyze and improve the impact of your digital strategy. FT Press.

[175] Jahan, M. S., & Martin, M. P. (2019). Exploring the Value of Your Website Analytics. *EPRA International Journal of Economic and Business Review, 4*(2), 66-69.

[176] Thoma, V., & Williams, B. (2009, August). Developing and validating personas in e-commerce: A heuristic approach. In *IFIP Conference on Human-Computer Interaction* (pp. 524-527). Springer, Berlin, Heidelberg.

[177] Ghoshal, S., & Westney, D. E. (1991). Organizing competitor analysis systems. *Strategic Management Journal, 12*(1), 17-31.

[178] Kong, R. (2017). 10 Step For Decreasing Ecommerce Cart Abandonment. Retrieved 20 October 2021, from https://www.bigcommerce.com/blog/abandoned-carts/#why-cart-abandonment-should-be-a-top-priority-for-online-retailers

[179] Local Consumer Review Survey: How Customer Reviews Affect Behavior. (2020). Retrieved 19 October 2021, from https://www.brightlocal.com/research/local-consumer-review-survey/

[180] Sabri Hassan Assaari, S. H. (2008). Evaluation of Factors That Increase Ecommerce Website Conversion Rates.

[181] Bradford, W. (2011). Reaching the Visual Learner: Teaching Property Through Art. Retrieved 19 October 2021, from https://papers.ssrn.com/sol3/papers.cfm?abstract_id=587201

[182] Visual content receives 94 percent more views than text-only marketing - PR Daily. (2017). Retrieved 19 October 2021, from https://www.prdaily.com/visual-content-receives-94-percent-more-views-than-text-only-marketing/

[183] (2021). Retrieved 19 October 2021, from https://www.nature.com/articles/s41467-019-09311-w.pdf

[184] (2021). Retrieved 19 October 2021, from https://unbounce.com/conversion-benchmark-report?_ga=2.254456456.1097472640.1632130861-815441142.1632130861

[185] The 100 Most Expensive Google AdWords Keywords. (2021). Retrieved 20 October 2021, from https://www.marketingprofs.com/charts/2016/30063/the-100-most-expensive-google-adwords-keywords

[186] Bradford, W. (2011). Reaching the Visual Learner: Teaching Property Through Art. Retrieved 20 October 2021, from https://papers.ssrn.com/sol3/papers.cfm?abstract_id=587201

[187] Rayson, S. (2015). Content, Shares, and Links: Insights from Analyzing 1 Million Articles. Retrieved 20 October 2021, from https://moz.com/blog/content-shares-and-links-insights-from-analyzing-1-million-articles

[188] How Helpful Is Live Chat? - eMarketer. (2021). Retrieved 20 October 2021, from https://www.emarketer.com/Article/How-Helpful-Live-Chat/1007235

[189] 44 Cart Abandonment Rate Statistics - Cart & Checkout - Baymard Institute. (2021). Retrieved 20 October 2021, from https://baymard.com/lists/cart-abandonment-rate

[190] Fox, M. (2015). Shopping Cart Abandonment: An $18 Billion Opportunity [New Ebook]. Retrieved 20 October 2021, from https://www.dynamicyield.com/blog/shopping-cart-abandonment-ebook-announcement/

[191] Remarketing: the Ultimate Guide for 2020 - GrowthBadger. (2019). Retrieved 20 October 2021, from https://growthbadger.com/remarketing/#chapter-6

[192] 44 Cart Abandonment Rate Statistics - Cart & Checkout - Baymard Institute. (2021). Retrieved 20 October 2021, from https://baymard.com/lists/cart-abandonment-rate

[193] 44 Cart Abandonment Rate Statistics - Cart & Checkout - Baymard Institute. (2021). Retrieved 20 October 2021, from https://baymard.com/lists/cart-abandonment-rate

[194] Checkout Optimization: 5 Ways to Minimize Form Fields in Checkout. (2021). Retrieved 20 October 2021, from https://baymard.com/blog/checkout-flow-average-form-fields